THE
RETURN

Book design by Jessika Hazelton
Printed in the United States of America
The Troy Book Makers • Troy, New York • thetroybookmakers.com

To order additional copies of this title,
contact your favorite local bookstore
or visit www.shoptbmbooks.com

ISBN: 978-1-61468-661-3

THE
RETURN

Bob Elmendorf

DEDICATION

Without the help and support of the following friends and relatives, these poems would never have been written. My Grandfather, George M. Elmendorf, who imparted a love of nature and travel. My father, George L. Elmendorf, who told the wife of SUNY Plattsburgh's President Dr. Angel that I was writing poetry and when she replied isn't that nice, maybe sometime he will write a sonnet, he countered, he's writing sonnets now. My mother, Jeanette H. Elmendorf who loved words, tutored me in Latin and my twin brother Peter Elmendorf who showed my early poems to his English teacher in Clarkson and supported me every step of the way as did his son Mark, who always knows what to say about them and his daughter Kristin Cimini who always takes time to say something encouraging about a poem. Karen Elmendorf for her beautiful gardens at camp.

Union College Professors: Hans Freund with whom I took seven courses and who was my mentor, Norman Johnson and Don Ross. Gary Fidel, Mike Turner, Jeff DeMunn, Tom Benedict, Jim Gallagher, Dave Demaine, Steve Radlauer, Dean Hoffman, Jon Littman, Bob Thurber, Peter Feldstein, Colin McGown, Phil Rice. Art Newgarden and Cynthia Newgarden, Joan Burke, David Hinsman and David Langdon. Members of Every Other Tuesday Poetry Workshop: Karin Maag-Tanchak, Tess Lecuyer, Lori Anderson Moseman, Sharon Stenson, Jill Hanifan, Sally Rhoades, Nancy Klepsch, Miriam Herrera, Darby Penny and Charlie Rossiter. Kinderhook Library Workshop: Karen Schoemer, Heather Moore Niver and Irene Mitchell. Dan Wilcox, Don Levy, Mary Panza. Joan Murray and her workshop: Heather Moore Niver, Maryanne Hammond, Laura Whalen, Lynette Noonan, Therese Broderick, Steve Almasi, Bunkong Tuon. The Howe Workshop. Jake Beauvais, Rich Robinson, Sue Oringle, Gina Qualliotine, Dee Duckworth, Sarah Miller, Nat Corwin, Sylvain Nagler, Bill Mancini, Dan and Emilie Michaud, Laura and Jeff Schwartzberg, Lucy Pracher, Nancy Smith, Wyn Hayes, Rebecca McBride, Dianne Leung, Anne Undeland, Mary Lou Peck, Jerry Pinto, Noel Werle, Lyle Jenks, Mark LaRiviere and Cathy Ramey, Noah Palmer,

Julia Rubel, Lilia Angello, my Latin students; Paul Novak, Nicole Furnee, Susan Davies, Nancy Rothman, Marcie Gardner, Herb and Elaine Ranney, Jens and Spee Braun, Pierre Douyon, Eric Braun, Ann Davidson, Sandy Beer, Christine Rosensteel, John Breasted, Chris Erb, Katherine Hughes, Susan Heins Rotelli, Jane Siegel, Susan R. Crabbe, Katherine Houk, Will Chamberlain, Bill and Bev Thompson, Wendy Dwyer, Ann Schillinger, Helen and Gene Braun, Regina Baird Haag, Dennis Haag, Chris DeRoller, Mike Clark, Ann Kjellberg, Phoenix Grace, Joseph Olejak, look at quaker directory, Elisabeth Grace, Ann Rommel, Linda Pagan, Maureen Aumand, Max Grieshaber and Susan Shaw, Jeannine Laverty, Jeanne Finley, Judy Elmendorf, Kevin and Diana O'brien, Sheela Rowland, Holly Montgomery, Ralph Blackwood, Peter Meixner, Heather Lloyd, Lee Jamison, Christian Sweningson, Richard Light, Mike Bouyea, Moreen Delbel Austin, Judy Beauvais, Jean Field, Kathy Manley, Dr. Rafil Dhafir, Buffy Curtis, Angelo Manno, Elizabeth Powers, Angela York Crane, Mardi Crawford, and Peter Kane Dufault.

CONTENTS

POPULATION EXPLOSION

The ironing board unfolds like a letter in a child's
alphabet, and lands like a stork in front
of the laundry. My mother bends down

in Chicago where my father inspects munitions
factories, salvages a sheet, billows it over
the board and flattens it against the grey padding.

The iron measures into the drift and out again
while my father on the outskirts of industrial
Chicago perambulates down boulevards

of grenades. Wrinkles on a sheet mark where
it would explode if it had a pin and powder.
My brother and I wait to be born invasion after invasion,

sigh over the islands, retreat from Japan.
My mother arranges winter in folds, shelves
them as if they were treaties. The board

flattens against the wall. A plane drones through
clouds. Dislodged, finned, black, nuclear, too
stunned to tumble, it exhumes a light too brilliant

for photography. The sprinkling bottle rests. Our
mother knew the end, undressed and submitted
while the burn wards around Hiroshima ran out of

gauze. The deliveries were on target.

IT'S TWINS

Before I thumped and was put in order
I was a plan in standing water
whose ripples repeated at the margins.

My lightning's static clicked in the stethoscope.
Over and over my skin like an envelope
sealed me for the salt in her arched canal.

Peter bumped me like a wandering buoy.
His unshut eyes winked goodbye at last.
He crept with his rope from our languid atoll.

Fish him said the nurse to the doctor.
But I heard the earth in the hoops of the latitudes,
so I stayed swallowed in the interior.

Safari of smiles at the watering hole.
Circles on targets graze their black range.
I want a sound not met by echoes.

Count grains and knots to get night on
the pine boards. Run your hand until
it topples into a groove. Push through

the groove. If I were. I were.
Fish him said the nurse to the doctor.
Vistas from the wave's escarpment
arranged desire. Me too please. Me too.

PARTHENOGENESIS

I divided the night into two pockets
leaving the one and entering the other.
I was electric in the dutch door socket.

I was the thread in the needle's rocket
that sewed the dusk and the dawn together.
I divided the night into two pockets,

meandered the seam that stitched charged crochets
switching cheeked hail in a thunder cloud's weather.
I was electric in the dutch door socket,

reversing the current in my two-pronged crotches
before I separated from my twin brother.
I divided the night into two pockets

and sired myself, no seed from dad's packet,
in a room of my own without mom's bother.
I was electric in the dutch door socket,

following the char that the lightning botched
into two terminals my acorn fathered.
I divided the night into two pockets.
I was electric in the Dutch door socket.

I DON'T NEED A CHOIR
TO SING A CHILD'S ANTHEM

I don't need a choir to sing a child's anthem
Get me a limp. I was hobbled enough.
Hang out a lantern and I'll return.

I don't need a choir to sing a child's anthem.
One lone song knows the flute's inside.
I am able to act myself. Fan out the toys.

I don't need a choir to sing a child's anthem.
Dirigibles in aquariums know their cue.
I'm just outside the Dutch door's bottom.

I don't need a choir to sing a child's anthem.
Take me by the hand. I've found my harmonica.
Sit in the circle. Roll me a ball.

I don't need a choir to sing a child's anthem.
I've sulked for three days. No food. On a pout.
My bed is my only companion.

I don't need a choir to sing a child's anthem.
I've got to give in, at least for now.
I'm no longer hungry but scared of all.

I don't need a choir to sing a child's anthem.
You welcome me back with soup and milk,
this animal back inside his whelk.

ABOVE THE TILLAGE
THE CHARM OF COOL STARS

Above the tillage the charm of cool stars
anoints with the light the small boy in the field,
and stammering out their praises he is far
from his birth and now he will not yield

to his mother so tender in the womb
roofed with stars and thick with coiling tubes.
The bumping of his brother nudged both to gloom.
The wind in her thrusting groins blew

both to light and snuffed the fetal darkness
from their eyes. Her calls came as crows
collect to hustle in the corn. Her caress
has jolted me between the rustling rows.

We robbed the fatal birthday of its wealth
which set two in motion when the want was one.
Could I have crept back in by some stealth
and left him to begin what we both have done?

I am the vassal of their ended growth.
They see their broken future whole in my eyes.
They played their future in a rolling couch,
and spend their fallow hopes in my small size.

SINISTER ET DEXTER

Two whelks recumbent on the ancestral shore
our beds were mirrored, mine on the right,
scooping up the tided night
animaled behind the bedroom door.

We pearled the grit that the breakers wore
styxed it to dreams by secret midnight,
or tossed in rough surf below the light
our columns thundering with nightmare's roar.

I tried his bed once when he was gone
sat on the transom and swung my legs left.
The knotty pine I almost stumbled upon
welling suddenly like discovered math,
described a solid's curves whose fathom
was unknown to me, my brother's path.

TELLING APART

I'm telling. You could hardly tell us
apart. We looked identical. Hey twin.
Picked last like the worst fruit
we stood in back the tallest split

to different teams. I'm falling apart.
Old shale buckling above a volcanic
cellar. Sharecropper miner of sedimentary
slag. Slate chattering down my side.

I'm a late bloomer obsidian finally
glassing my station. Bonafide. Hedge
out of the roundhouse low squat with
a loco motive. Out of our munificence

we have given you a childhood to earn,
to fail minima cum laude. I am bored mortar
to fly my parent's pennants in, my
magma charta bumps as it cools, a driveway
they can park their Chrysler on.

ALLEE ALLEE IN FREE

At my windows the stars appear,
playmates who won't ring the doorbell.
The girl who just moved in is there as well
her blue eyes distant but clear.

The cloud boys are with them ready to veer
from pane to pane even down to the sill,
and the cross lot planets who raise hell
swaggered up from the horizon's grenadiers.

So it's hide and seek and the maple is home.
Sick, punished or curfewed I watch from my bed,
she counts to a hundred out loud and alone
while a boy hisses a girl to the hedge.
She's behind the tree where the marbles are thrown.
No, she's doffing her stars. She's caught me instead.

THE TWINS' CHILD BRIDES

Our first visitors at our playhouse were Suellen
and Jane, whom we met in kindergarten
and who used to tease us when on restriction
in our yard. Two six year old sirens
would call to us from the margins.

Jane lived on broad street and we pledged
to marry. Suellen's home almost edged
on ours, just cross lots from Schlesinger's.
She was a tomboy, her mom a swimmer,
her dad a doctor, her brother an Olympian.

Too young to know what we were missing,
we were left to our own devices unchaperoned.
The wind in the ash arcade did all the kissing.
Hands held were not ours. Persephones,
they went underground until our first reunion

where Suellen confided she had taken heroin,
and perhaps I had rejoined about asylums
I had been locked up in for manic-depression.
Jane chaired the second reunion.
Pete and I did not stay for the dance.

THE ICICLISTS

In every elementary school winter,
centuries of constellations lowering
star by star, frost's livery, dammed splinters
siphoned from the drip edge. We glowered

in prison behind them, February's wards.
A rack of ice, a portcullis. We castled, nobles
back of a rank of pawns, undrawn wells
gargoyled from a parapet into centaurs.

Sweated beads, creweled on translucence,
Orion the growing dark with forms of myth.
We step from stage left and right to fence
with shards. We're celestial monoliths.
Melting and on the way home silent,
cold, wet, late, hungry but still Lapiths.

CATARACT

Antecedent Venus and the moon in the blue West
sailing from tree to tree address me rurally. A lunar
intraocular lens transplant will occur in March.
Soon my pool will blink from rain. The portcullis

will be lifted and the lattice shadowing
the garden will be folded up, a collapsible ruler.
My lid's an observatory's rind. The moon's
spreading batter across its griddle. Will I

be young again, even before I had glasses,
standing at the stove with my plate out,
the almost empty pitcher dripping two silver
coins, small change but welcome.

THE TERRIBLE GOLD
THAT GLOWS WITH A SHUDDER

The terrible gold that glows with a shudder
rejects the upper jeweler and his tongs.
The molds that steer the liquid like a rudder
derail down there the notes from lines of song.

My mother's golden notes above the mantel
confine a tune that has risen from below.
The wax that withers down the shrinking candle
conducts the flame where fleet forms flow.

The cinders from the hearth are clinked to cellars
where the vestments of the goddesses are thumped.
The infernal manual is a stuttering speller,
whose prediction that the moon will be clumped

with another moon that makes the night waves slap,
raises the braille in the dreams I tap.

DIVISION

My mom had no room of her own unless
you count the basement laundry where
she kept her girlhood scrapbooks we made
her thumb through. This was over balanced
by dad's workshop with its bench stretching
out of my reach into an alcove of screws,
the curled snail plane under the level's
horizon, a quorum of drills, and the miter
box's crossing. She had, however, secured
a space over the whatnot whose drawers
we found our allowance in. On a grid
of finishing nails a claque of trivets
roosted, taxidermized grackles, foundry
names championed on their borders, a rail
to catch the sad iron, heavy, hot and
husbanded.

I GRIP THE TURNING KNOB
AND AM BURNED BY BRASS

I grip the turning knob and am burned by brass
whose smoking bolt has felt a heavier hand.
The portal's panes divide the light and sand,
and sulphur reeks through where I meant to pass.
But I would go to where I had been last,
if only to explore my underland.
All frazzled tresses, she commands
the gap that sparks in place of glass.

I am shot as a mountain volt through clouds
and shake to hear behind my thunderclap.
I storm over my past and send loud
hail, waking my mother from a summer nap,
and wash the verdure from her glass shroud
to watch my birth beneath her valley lap.

BROTHERS

The shelves that flanked the stairs are empty now,
so close to the door where Wee Willie knocked.
Retreating footsteps brought the thoughts of sleep.

The rapping on the wall curtailed our play.
The fingering shadows splayed against the ceiling
Fell within to darkness that held the corners.

The silhouette of sleep appears tonight.
Twin shadows vie for mastery of the light.

PATER NOSTER

I've forgotten how I knew it was the night,
but approaching footsteps followed by a knock
told us he'd come, who turning left, then right,
would instruct our souls that could not fly, in flight.

The Pater Noster that we'd memorized,
he brought in a book to my brother's bed,
and sitting on the wide rail that ran beside,
with each sentence he filled his head,
until the words took meaning in their tide.

And I was next who'd heard the broken prayer,
though I kept myself hidden from his point of view,
with maybe just a look or two
across to my brother and his sayer
who held in thought what I was now to do.

When the prayer was over and the text was closed,
from my walled in bed her rose,
ascended the stairs and shut the door,
more alone than ever before.

THE QUARRY

abandoned near the river
my father siphoned. He unlocked
the deep quadratures of water
and beguiled them with lunes.
I knew early on he had a way with
it. The chamois that he dragged
across the car hood got what
he was after. Sprinklers performed
for him. Even the Spring basement
flood left him with its catch
of worms waterlogged and flaccid.
So this moat was no challenge.
Down the sleepy ranks of stone
he lowered the level. He exposed
tables and benchmarks of a
subaqueous order. Dark green
formations grew statelier from
his reversing Nile. In his den
he showed customers slides
on a projector, monuments pensively
recalling their submersion.
In a store, diner and house I've
peered into tables and countertops
finished with this granite, and
in its crystals I took the color
blindness test, almost making out
his face in the feldspar.

THE MARBLE PIT

The Douglas brothers brought bags of agates,
cats' eyes, purees and blundering puckers
to our hole with its tamped circle
between the hatchway and the cedar hedge.

My twin and I played together,
if his wasn't closest then mine might be,
and we merged our winnings,
running the dirt off under the faucet,
drying them in packs.

The older Douglas brother said
it wasn't fair to the rest of them,
our gang of two lightening their sacks,
emptying their cans.

We promised to keep our takings separate
but to ourselves we swore to blend our treasuries.
We played, each a god beside the other,
guised as a familiar mortal,
nudging a close shot of our opponent's away,
crowding the hole with each other's allies.

Double monarchs of an empire of glass,
we tandem demoned the best of their rolls
and damned their marbles to our repositories.
In prayer I still turn to my fraternal other,
for an unwavering hand to follow
his almost deciding throw,
our new foes confounded by our old alliance.

YELLOW DOMINO

I'm the last played. Remnant from an old box
I sub for the one behind the radiator.
Jaundiced ivory, I sit back in the pile,
not picked not picked while a jaunty low
number butts head-to-head and waves its tail
pleading at the end of the chain for a Dutch door
three. My double six can match elevator braille,
and radio broadcast lights boxed. I'm drawn
from two dies with uncut corners. I won't fix
my Styx eyes, alabaster body. My last trick
will equal their best and call for the same.

NORTHWEST PASSAGE

My brother and I are reading
in easy chairs, my uncle at his desk,
my aunt with a book. We're spread out

in the after dusk in furniture
the color of the deer we visit in a meadow.
An absorbed silence spreads like strawberries,

sturdied with a clock condensing seconds
like a lemonade glass, backed up
by the grandfather's bass on the landing.

Quarried slate tips the sidewalk around the corner
that rustling maples shade for moss
on the sedimentary basement.

The mountains have blocked the street ends,
pulled on shadows for pajamas.
Home is a weak light mist happily obscures.

THE OPHTHALMOLOGIST

Delivered to a room darkened with drawn blinds,
brown wood, green walls and softened by rugs,
before a white screen with a chart of five black letters
which is not the typewriter's order nor the periodic
table of elements, nor alphabetical, but lower case,
vowel heavy, letters mostly without stems,
and not a word in any language known to me,
the same every year and each eye has to try
it alone and each row is more difficult, like footnotes,
even though it's boxed in its own rectangle of light.
Finally I fail and resort to guessing some, but he shows
a smaller row each time until it's all speculation.
Partial eclipses of the sun instrument my appointment.
Look to the left corner, to the right, look up, look down.
The lenses of the clouds click over the eye of the moon.
Better or worse. He slides them in a ladder
like a rack of suns depicting its solstitial journey
across the heavens. I worry about
which one to choose, afraid of ending up
with the wrong prescription.
But who chose the brightness of our sun for life,
pulled the moon in close to us at night
and sewed a sack of stars to steer our journeys by,
loads me with calm, and I don dark glasses
for driving home.

TIME

Whitening like the neurologist's light
steady in my eye, hold it, good, as close
as that, the room darkened, the florescent
hallway through the door she parted her teeth
enamel panels parking a tongue behind
her hair dry and fortyish high browed no scent
a smile quickened at the end of some sentences
her pen in a small hand recording my burden.
I'd unfolded a paper smock with ties under
it had it on backwards, reversed it
at her direction and tore it. At home time
came up to my feet and burned, an animal
condemned to infancy, whose appetite
I could neither solace, fuel nor quench.

BEFORE I LEARNED TO FLY

I'd run to the edge of my tether, teacher air
brushing at my legs and slide the horizon
under me. Where was speed to propel me,
and the faith to remain airborne? I wanted
to elope with a night tarred and feathered
with birds, to ogle the cold marble moon
exchanged for the pucker sun. Stars
would be my flying instruments, warm
ones over Florida dipping in arcs to reach
the lagoons. I'd sew the coast line, zipped
by the unbundling wave. And doze
until Cuba, my wings breathing in lungs
of air. Every evening started with a dream,
and sleep ended steadier and surer. Morning
I rose, walked quickly, skipped and dove
into the tide of air and felt it pull me round
the globe and peel me to the heavens,
where hand sized galaxies turned stars
as thick as whirlpools.

THE NATURALIST

Collecting myself from glass, rock and shell,
bringing together what once were lost,
I have my room at every angle crossed
with objects whose being I cannot quell.

Each shelf is loaded with nut and fossil,
throwing off a darkness that chills like frost,
or rife with roots some great tree tossed
that stopped the lightning before it fell.

I use crystals in place of a level,
pyrite's my plumb, fungus my arc.
The house that I'm building is all internal,
the whelk is my square, pollen my chalk.
Deeper than whirlpools toward the infernal,
old snails spin at the pace of a walk.

TO THE NEW OWNER

There is no part of house, hedge or lot
that I have not known by mind or pulse.
Stand anywhere and on the spot
I've stood, stooped and knelt.
Try the gardens with an unpracticed look,
reviewing first the tulip's twisting scarves;
there I have studied what the short sun took
and turned to figures his long rays carve.
You won't be prisoner of the circling grain,
the waters in the knots and the wall's brooks
won't run for you. Though you glance again,
where shelves were will just be space for books.
But share with us one similarity:
the too deeply planted crocus again won't be.

OLD IRON FOUND IN A RIVER POTHOLE

Rust and corrosion are things of the past.
This kidney shaped slag's pockmarks were bubbles
in the molten ore not a current's troubles
wormed into an ugly piece of ballast.

Too misshapen even for Hephaestus' last,
you clubfooted deep into unshoveled gravel,
root, trowel, weight, meteor, cinder, tuber,
seer's map of the future's topography.

I am now ready to die by example.
Palmed, backwatered orphan, nostrils
and eyes enough for three skulls,
you'll be my coffin plate, your forehead ample
as a squid's, so figure to skulk
over a maze of bones, my final sculpture.

DIAMOND LOVER

Two acute and two obtuse angles oblonged
into foundry iron, poker end, equilibrium,
sunken flag, magnet's target, effluvium
of the river discarded, wronged

into the pothole, scouring rhombus song
mingled with adamants scraped in a drum
of granites, garnets, quartz, gneiss, glum
sandstones, ground glass, coins, rings, strong

spikes square cut, things a long way from home.
Your clumsy bevel's rounded by this pocket's change,
points no longer cardinal, a compass none
could steer by but find himself with its cold flange
in a country of froth, pitch and thrum
where swallowed medicine increases the pain.

THE JACKDAW PAIR

We do not snub the fringes of the river
but along its banks hunt up the pebbled shoals
for treasures to line our nests with.
Iron brilliant and mirrory beneath rust
turns in its original angle from the forge,
while the river chilled
from wading through snow fields
rises and drops like mercury,
and bumps glass spalls into necklaces.
Cup fungi abacus bark
whose sums thrill from so much addition.
Quartz unobscures toward crystal.
The sun slides, a sturgeon above clouds
one forecast away from us,
its gilt belly an iris of promises.
Across the river a dog howls,
so we flap to another beach,
and cross our beaks over the semi-literate sand,
printed with the meander of animals.

THE WALKER

Sitting in my driveway snugged up
behind my car she finally turned the ignition
off and talked with the duration of a comet
and the speed of a shooting star. Another,
when I couldn't drive, would pull over
with me to inspect the latest wildflower
coloring the roadside. We taught each other
and wondered at the rest. Butter and eggs,
its spire top clubbing blossoms, seemed
early as did many, a childhood sunset at 8 PM
when I was sent to bed in daylight. I am
a quadrangle in a patch of wood and houses.
I tire at three miles and wait to be driven
further. Who will bring me the first local
peaches? Old friends gone whom I could walk
the river with, to look for a companion
to a scrubbed green glass shard. Whom could
I delay with such a foolish errand for verdant
translucencies, whose children wait at home,
whose jobs call and husbands. I put on hold
many favorite journeys and learn to know
and love a tract I'd walked too fast through.
Mercurial I poked a turtle tucked at both ends,
stranded, off the asphalt into the weeds.
I drooped dead snakes over my walking stick
and bedded them in the grasses. I carried
a wounded gray and yellow bird with red hash
marks to the bushes to what end I could not tell.
I found an oriole, its grandeur on tarmac.
A gray heron among the altitudes of trees
flew just fast enough to keep itself aloft
and blood red mushrooms pushed their round
caps through a skin of leaves by a marsh seeded
with green algae.

THE FOUNDLING

Set on a ledge by the side of a brook just
above the flume a pothole crammed full
of stone rests in a time of low waters.
A brackish meniscus stretches across the top
recording on the uncalibrated side the daily
rainfall let down by the conifers. I sit
beside it as if at a well and pluck a few stray
pebbles out of the lip and try to move the next.
Stuck. I start to work with a stick and wedge
it out. Sand clings to its sides a little cool
from the water. Smells like a congested swamp.
The stone is harder than buttocks but as smooth.
I dig though a juggle of stones until I
hit bottom, but no, it's a hemisphere. When
I remove this plug stones important
as viscera hump their shapes into my palm.
I've got enough for an oracle but keep going
into the black blue gray area, stones almost
porous now in the water longer than mermen,
pull out two almost keepers, from the gullet,
and then one nuzzles my fingers, cranes for my hand,
cold, smooth, compact, a pleasurable density
and in the light the prize of the cavity, striated
with tilted off-white clouds, mottled in the tropic
of cancer, a soft and deliberate planet. Further I
scrape gravel, a plural of stones. I am up
to my shoulder in it and can reach no further.
I leave the mortar to its pestle of water and stone,
wishing it high waters and the right sized stones.

AGAINST SLEEP'S GYMNASTS
IN THE NEXT ROOM OVER

tumbling toward their exit, waking a trail
of postures, a vein of bumpy interlocked concretions,
pantomiming a swimmer's sloughed somersaults,
I jackstraw last night's dishes
from the drain board, platter them into cupboards.
The plates loll like a stranded school of moons,
watch dials time no longer crosses. The forks
rise in the silver chest abandoning their seconds.
The knives roost in their pockets standing up
the hours. Birds strum the badminton
guy wires, beak the string straggling
off a tent stake and fly it taut, whirring
that radius into a hundred circles. A quaternity
of plums lies in a white bowl geared blue enough
to cog. Polygamous, I watched all of them.
Plucked from the tree's orrery, these blue-black planets,
finished with the sheen of our millennia,
are viscera, the tree's unstomached innards,
as ripe with prophecy as animal entrails.
Their buttocked lobes cock a purple contour.
Fugitives from the stand's phalanx,
they rub against each other, stones in a pothole,
deepening it while diminishing themselves. I
turn one over; its seam curves like a scythe.
It's most like my thumb, blunt yet purposeful.
Let them stand for themselves and the three
incidents above already ripening into memories,
crossing the borders with an agent's stealth,
silhouettes robbing palettes of their colors,
trading at night rates on the exchange of dreams.

HIP BOOTS

Two footsteps lengthened out of dark
hung from the cellar rafters stranded
waders stayed there years jumped into
by nightmares to ride the black

o'clocks. These were the overseer's
a noise behind me a grip at the base
of the spine I could not throw. Bossed
by deep water the stream's muscles

tightening for a dunk I lost my
breath asleep and gulped bulged
draughts unexpelled unbalanced floated
to the next flume's cough feet stamped

kicked into a rapid's braids a jack
of water sheathing to my crotch.

THE PATH

I laid shale stones in a field of cobble
lowering them in water until they struck
the sediment table, their sudden loss of weight
from the reduced gravity in dreams. Soon
I was under too, using their heft until
I had them level, straightening the path
with my eye alone so I could walk it
even if blurred by waves. Each was flat
and wide as my foot and set side wise
to help if I got knocked off balance.
I stopped at where I would start to swim,
and from this quarried stair regarded
the gently sloping shore, the beach where packs
of broken ledge and rounded shales pocketed
gravels and silt and where the ice pushes
to solve the beach's tireless puzzle. The water
stilled and I could see my stride blocks, steps
deepening to me, and all the till they crunched in,
with quartz, marl and calcite. I turned to the bay
of the lake its scooped shore miles across
and then out to the lake itself which ran
from Saint-Jean-Sur-Richelieu, to Whitehall.
I was cut in half by the water, a level's bubble
set in my navel. I was blued and whitened
by the sky. Sturgeon grounded in the bottom's
current in the lake's middle. And just ahead was
the eel, an untrained vine, hanging a letter
outside the alphabet, and before it started
to squirm, I backed away from this aqueous
caduceus, sucker demon, a worm to save for graves.

BLUE MOON

Two this July one on the first and one at the end.
The pool where I used to swim in the Kinderhook
so long and deep, had a waterfall at its entrance
and exit, but when the river flooded it took these
out and the silver water color fled and then I left.
No more swimming up to the mouth of the pool.
No more drifting to its lower falls over a scrubbed
bottom of stones, the trees overhanging its banks
with their canopy of shade marking their surfaces
until green & black overlapped in summer's teens.
I am not climbing down the steep bank a meadow
ended after a sweet trudge on a path of grasses,
or cooled refreshed shaking the water droplets off
to make my verdant way along the river turning
and widening and narrowing dividing into channels
sounding over a short fall or segregating an island.
Help me a sublunarian get to the end of this month.

SAND

Don't sieve me. Let me go back to the boulder
where you can guess me wrongly.
Run your hand along my smooth hide.
Lichen badges, land masses globes map.
Promote me. I can shift for myself.
Petered out in pebbles I'd be spent,
pennies in a candy store, dispersed as ashes.
I want to be my own monument,
not dropped undammed from a plane
or lagged in an esker.
I'm not a horn that spills its bounty in October.
Iceberg, whale, elephant I'm diving,
the elevator's waist has dropped below the floor,
a grey room you'll not go in. No Jonahs.
But I'll lift you up and from my back
you'll feel the surge you've scrambled to,
mineral veins rain can't weather,
scars at my rounding.
Don't disturb me with hammers.
I slide a wide shadow over five o'clock flowers.
I'm a crude gnomon. I am. I am.

SOLSTICE

I hide in words. That's not where you'll catch me.
Winter, your first sun ducking through the woods
drops in a well at four, a perfect match for me.

A December maple rounded in fog watches me
from a field of snow, just where I'd have stood.
I hide in words. That's not where you'll catch me.

In this poem you'll find my photograph, scree
at the cliff's bottom, I've done all I could,
drop in a well at four, a perfect match for me.

Or let's settle on a glacial erratic, free
standing on a ledge's rim by granite troughs
whose loose pink feldspar oblongs weather roughly.
I hide in words. That's not where you'll catch me,

better try a school of gravel, a swatch, warily
under current, organized against the flow.
Drop in a well at four, a perfect match for me.

But best of all the math in sand candidly
pouring homeless on the beach. Should
I hide in words, that's not where you'll catch me,
drop in a well at four, a perfect match for me.

THE SOLARIUM

Conducting the sun through its seasonal
declensions, you steadfastly record
on your graduated plate, scored
by the gnomon's profile, a reasonable

interpretation of locally made time.
I often see you silent in a garden,
needing no lovers' pardon
for wearing every shadow without chimes.

You mime the hours with unsignaled quarters,
and make them both unconscious of their bliss,
by laying hour next to hour with a shadow's mortar
until the last rays reluctantly miss

the triangle, now waiting above its dial
for another sun and its sliding hours to while.

CRABAPPLE

Stopped by the tangle of your branches
in a thicket by the pond side, I hear
the spring Phoebe, and the gray wind,
behind ripples, shifting with each pass.
Several weeks from bees, I await your blossoms.
It has been a year since I last sat on this bench,
trammeling myself in your vine's script,
making a decision at each of your forks.
Now the ripples zebra to the shore,
erasing themselves for another pattern,
while the cold earth releases its first scents.

UNPICKED

We who are no longer quite young
though still bright and not yet fallen,
feel in the wind a distant autumn
and hear in the stream another tongue.

Footsteps near us rung by rung,
bees have long since left our pollen,
and grey ladders are tall when
they rest in forks where we are strung.

Frost will have its laces hung
on wide green glades. The shadow's drawing,
the sap finally in November stalling
strand some fruit above each trunk.

And drifts the wind around us will have flung
will be warm as robes as those winds worsen
and soon we'll see the snow fields glisten
from sun and moon and moon and sun.

THE PRESS OF WEEDS TURNS BLACK

The press of weeds turns black, the moon
    goes shallow, the wet wind easily in bare limbs fits,
    the drowsy wasp in the corner flits,
the sun and his lengthening shadows set too soon.
All's stopped, in march light to resume
    the seed's progress, and where the bright moss quit
    another border with flowers will sit,
softening its boulder, brightening its noon.

Fortunate apples, the meadow is yours alone.
    Loosened in liquor, the flesh within your robes
will be the first food for your emptied stones.
    Plot an orchard topped with lifted globes.
Late next autumn you'll still have to show
another unreachable, reddening cargo.

FALSE SPRING

The crocus cast a long root and snared a shaft
but a storm came and buried it in snow.
Then sun and rain melted that to tallow
until clouds dumped sleet on nature's craft.

Such false springs cannot be paramours. Aft
are fecund confreres and their colorful fellows,
and underground garden's greens that go to yellow
when blighted from the sun behind the cloud raft.

Still the vernal theme is carried by the brooks,
or on the breasts of the Apriled finches.
The muskrats dive in ponds to mud their stooks
when snakes under the flatiron rocks are wrinkling.
The geese's wings are pages in my book
rising and falling, lifting the stars by inches.

MARCH

This is the month in which Spring begins
stored near the end in the candle's ankle,
shucking its days which like brook lids blanket
the current paused in bulbs curved and pagan.
It raises the level of days in its basin
laying hopes like leaves upon its banks,
passing a storm white flame within its ranks
until indigo elides in a gelid spectrum
the pallors assembled as winter's tinctures
whose scattered palette has clipped the brush of frost.
toppled ice wands, welded on a pool, blink. Sure
shards collapse in a blue blur. More melt and are lost.
The dulled, scuffed skates the buckled rink's lure
cannot attract keep rouge off cheeks that blushes now accost.

APRIL

I read a line of trees at the foot of the hill,
once the indecipherable alphabet of childhood,
that spelled out not their names but shapes in grays
and browns, an entanglement of boughs
fanning to their tops. I'm long finished with genus
and species. I never saw the double of an elm,
limbs dividing until its form is freed. Its speech
conned from the meadow's hornbook, whispers
me down the road, the vigor of a March brook
in colloquy with a wind at the crossroads. The sun
and I walk down to the river hand in hand,
the earth's scent still stoppered. Next to walls
the spears of flowers thrive, their blooms
unfurled, timed by the same clock as love.

BALLET

I am a glove turned inside out
a weather vane drunk on the wind
the day has been prancing beside me
postillion at a midnight billet
false started by a flash of a thousand stars
I've lost my shadow at the moon's tag sale
look for my recorder where I sea crashed
I've become the consort of mermaids
join me in the delirium of sleep
bringing your pajamas of dreams
I have a journey no map can keep
secrets that burst at the seams
maned I graze the breeze fed meadows
stand four legged by a brook to dip my head
my royal lineage is the trillium's
and I vary as a mockingbird
close the book on a golden prayer
and your lips on a hopeful song
I am an unaccompanied player
on a piano black octaves long

MY LODGER

Ravens prospecting a snowless hill avoid
the drummed hay, and peck at the summary of bugs
graded by the combing wind in the yellow grasses.

They do the arithmetic in the straw
ticking off the suns in a warm January,
stationing themselves, calendar numerals,

brands, irons, stowing the hours like a tan.
Out of work by choice now seven months
my lodger has called me manic. And so

I must appear, busy on the weekends
to rest from work, but I remember manic
and when my back was good laying up

wall with my wife, a spate of limestone,
a soliloquy of flat capstones.
He's entered in the pasture's ledger, sibilant

decimal, strident in June, agile enough
to dodge the maws of bitter February.

NOAH

Snow wearing the paint at the ends of porches
settles down forever in the cracks of the boards.
Winter in February is still walking towards
icicles held aloft as artic torches.

Ice bibs the shingles in their rumpled courses,
wet wood is warping in the attic's wards.
A dry wind is rattling the meadow's gourds
at split ice fording the stream at its sources.

If I in search of thaw should free a dove
at the first budded branch it would stop,
and bring back its quarry to my outstretched glove;
then why restive watch these drifted banks as drop
by drop they lower water from above?
Put on their patience. The wait for spring with love.

THE RETURN

The thump of flames in the iron blue stove
swimming like goldfish in orange bars
of the spectrum is the sound of blankets
shaken over a camp bed in early spring.

White grass goes on and off like the basement
socket over a storm of tools and dead lanterns.
I preview stonewalls clean as curbs, waiting
for the light to change, embarrass foundations

of barren field stone. Tugged weeds
and pebbled shoals glint with pockmarked
glass sundered from a lost dump. Litter
of paper birches, cursive ferns,

night wind cupping the fahrenheit, orientals
rolled in purple trillium, a settlement
of cones, unwrinkling rhubarb, truculent octaves
of the wintered piano, bark unwinding from

the porch's cedar columns, an increase in insects,
repose of the stored shutters, downspout's
treasures, snow flattened leaves, wheelbarrow's
creak and the calligraphy of moles.

THE INTERLOPER

Night is an interrogative. The owl's questions
float in the glen where shadows voiced
by the articulate moon stilt their own ground,
measure the trees for graves. The back
of the interrogatory toad bunched in field grass
fouls with its scrawled lozengy
my push for ornament, my desire to align.
Leaves in conclaves ask what will I do in life
after goodbyeing twilight and joining their elopement.
I lie in new milkweed troweling out of zigzagged straw.
The butterflies and blooms aren't back yet
nor are my hands stained from opened pods,
but their seeds will include me in their count.

BREEZE

Incurable tempest that livens up to rage,
drop your snatched umbrellas near the bright
rain boots and shake your slicker right
where you are. Wear clouds low and wage
a war of weathers that change too fast to age.
With bellows swell the scurrying kite
until its broken girdle hurls out of sight.
Build with four winds the crossed vane's cage.
Stoop to ruffle a steeple's shingles then fly
through the hanging laundry's harp. Here
in the side yard, scattering leaves large and dry,
you'll cut a corner fast enough to sheer
holly hocks whose pink lusters you bluster by.
Now you've come with wings spread so near,
ray or condor, that papers capsize
or spread their pages to clear
the ground and rise, rustling with a sigh,
in a lover's grasp transported to old years.
Two dresses are next. Already high,
the hems are raised in front and rear
until the following boys descry
the anatomies of love and fear.
We need no sock or four cupped gauge
to measure what the flurrying branches cite.
We gasp when off a hill you set the stage
by blowing out the stars with clouds. Some nights
you kneel among the grasses and persuade
the tops of plants to shed their seeds in flight,
or coax the shutters with ghost, gust or shade
to raise with their rhythms the first grey light.

THE PHOTOGRAPHER

At the end of December you shudder
through the forest hungry for light
on your pools and rapids
silvered with mercury, slough frost
to tint a scale one wind from ice.
Pewter ewers no sideboard has contained
fill whose greens have gone to grey.
You stop at bends, stilled by a pool,
late-afternoon the unbroken winter clouds
into blue slide shows, silver-chest their oddities.
You are my treasury, I can't skewer
light, pin it dripping from the tray,
trashed cumulus pocketed in whirlpools,
a stratus dunked in ripples. Darkroom swindler,
you heist the joints of clouds to marble
your meanders, click away, it's just past
winter and the diluted sun can still
unfilm your icing pools to be caught
there, a welcome intruder.

WONDER BEYOND KNOWLEDGE

The rainbow is interrupted by analysis.
We compute its product and put it on a chart.
Each bird that sings is known in every part.
Their wings move like levers in paralysis.
Long shells' dipped curves lose to ellipsis
their coral abandon before they start.
Snakes seethe, their mortal tongues dart,
but ask their velocity before they hiss.
Flowers bloom again in perfume's vials,
petals split to shed a vital scent.
Each day the sun in winter indents
a paragraph, static on our radio dials.
We know the wattage of the filaments
of mushrooms, the volume of the firmament.
But star fire spilling just outside the tent
pools in dreams and the tabloid moon, spent,
dips below the west like a ladle, while
round owls from the twilight's sacrament
fly onto branches that growth has bent
over a stream grinding an ancient aisle.
The candle yellow flowers of spring wish
another bright year along the water;
this fall over a foot of stone and farther
up another brims a pool where pebbles wash;
blue green mountains undulate, twist
into passes, spill valleys and brought
boulders hold, piled in the throats of gorges,
got by a glacier on evenings much like this.

WONDER

A maple admits more than my mind holds
of starlight, whose harp limbs bow
too sharp for panes.

Beyond my sight starry windows elude
with curves the glazier's hand.
The black frames open

all around to the rippling wind,
snagging in billows like hot glass.

Grouped in new shapes, the distorted
stars sag. Blown about the crown,
I climb from their wavy blue light,
heading for shutters and no fire.

EARTH

Your starfished shores and woods crackling
with snails, brook pools' radii trout try,
nests forked in the beech elephanting
below, meteor midden, chopsticked

by lightning, storm ridden, sanskritted
with hedges, troughed with canyons,
sand sieved, lakes extracting blue sky dyes,
brush snake trailed and full of fox tricks.

I am black slag glassed from lava
still too hot to touch, reheated star ruin,
nebula sediment a god has not nodded over
whose perfumed locks I'd be immune
to, left out of the above octave,
waiting for a beach of my own.

CHANGE OF HEART

The world is flat. After the rain I'd plot
my course from puddle to puddle,
bend over to dwell in one for a while,
my local newspaper. The sun was
headlined, but I was a major story
descending in sometimes rippling columns.

I could sleep on the solid ones that had
changed to mirrors, even in August
a cool glass under my cheek, a summer
nap of Pan, laying down my tubes
I made change with, an unslung quiver,
sharps protruding. I was your substitute

and would wake at night under
the staveless stars, collect myself, charge
time and pipe a beginning before numbers
and alphabets, a hurdy-gurdy man, alone
in the cedars, worrying a moon over their
tips, scarving a mist from the country.

NO MOON

Somewhere under the bedcovers of another's
sky you set, spent from lavishing light
the color of dairies on a darkened earth.

I tally the queer luminosities of stars
greedily bleaching a night without you.
The parched glass burns hours of grains in its throat, salt

clogged in the cap of the milky way.
They keep their distance and I am waves backed
up in front of sand castles, dry towers

who would want to sift when wet. I'm a moat,
a tidal square, a water rook hunting for basements,
shallow well with a bottom for pennies, a surface

where planets and moons may come. I can
be still and dark enough for stars. Cistern
rounding drops from a lesson of slates,

could you encompass or endure such
panoply or would you quench the embers as
a stream, or wink startling into consternation
cold signs of love: math held in chalk.

THE MONOLOGUE

A wan January day kicked up a few pinks
that got behind the trees in back of the snow
and salmoned us into evening. Descending
a sanded dirt road heeling behind, I thought
we'd have some colloquy but he told
stories that lengthened and thickened
the closer we got to home. If I paused even
in mid-sentence I was interrupted, a branch's
perch borrowed by a vine. I was looking for
an orphic mirror drinking its own water,
a stingy hydrant's unplumbed ready flow,
a storm sewered drain sworn in by spring
downpours, a centaur leading me to drink,
hooves, mane and tail cut out by Matisse.

SOMEWHERE BETWEEN
THE STARS AND SNAILS

Somewhere between the stars and snails
still coiled in the shape of the univalve's worm
without a shell I raise these sheets for sails.

Cygnus no longer needs a string. Her pale
wings glide steadily above the storms.
Somewhere between the stars and snails

even on the horizon where distance fails
I have no prominence. Below waves fish swarm.
Without a shell I raise these sheets for sails,

dragging my anchor in a strangling gale.
I am a clay heaven, dropped earth still warm,
somewhere between the stars and snails.

In tow I glide on another's trail.
The hawk's shadow is ahead of it like harm.
Without a shell I raise these sheets for sails,

and in the unforgiving dark watch them go pale.
I want to put on my old uniform.
Somewhere between the stars and snails
without a shell I raise these sheets for sails.

THE RITE OF AUGUST

Losing the path in a field of nettles and briars
I cede my steps to the next wanderer
and whipped by raspberries scratch
back to the wood's needled ground,
the grove of apple trees, the boulder's fane,
to meet the rill that solves the meadow,
I the minotaur that could not stumble into Eden,
pacing outside that labyrinth's dozened streets.

DEATH OF A POET

It was not for want of water that I fell
drops silvering an already silver pool,
nor a mirror's beveled shore after a rule
of wind. Not tide that made such a swell

I was buoyant and no wave could quell
my swimming. And not the newel
post turning on a landing wide and cruel
with life I'd thrown a line to. I cannot tell,

the music changes key, my evening's colors
grade from style to style without rest.
The shoal's chattering stones repeat my dolor.
I am amphibious with death
and will be infinity's suitor,
unburdened of my heart and breath.

ICARUS AFTER THE FALL

I wore my pelt scuffling in the gravel,
my left side carded to the nap, sans
hands, feet and head. I am a discard,
a failure of myth, destitute in a quarry,
yarn bargained out of stars, a shroud weave,
a chalk lined crime scene, look up
to where I was, a grave plotted by
the cornerstones of Orion.

WHOSE HAND IS ON
MY PEN WITH MINE

Whose hand is on my pen with mine,
looping cursives, guiding me through
another's alphabet, foreign as the palmer
method. Runes, tusks, vines, roots

shake out of the rope and lasso
my consonants. Hastate hedge,
and brook script, stenography
of vines, briar short hand, a juniper's

calligraphy, characters drifting in
like clouds. Lapsa lingua, weeds
in my garden, choke my crop
of words, the tabula rasa a clay

wet with Semitics, stars ahead of
my hand, my pen a sparkler,
a baton in the night trying
to catch up with the fireflies.

SECOND STORY MAN

I don't need ladders. I'm not on the level.
Stilted letter stalked across the page.
It's not your jewelry that I'm after
but a circadian language,

the rising of the stars tattooed
on your windowpanes, the intake
of the wind parting curtains so wooed
their folds tremble like a fern brake.

The funereal dove, the pull of winter,
the night cured to a rind of sunrise,
a citrus moon low in the West's drink,
heat leaving the house unsatisfied.

ORNATE INDULGENCE
IN BIZARRE DESIGN

Ornate indulgence in bizarre design
brambles the framework like an axiomed briar,
as if a raveling cable's wires
invented geometries to define
the intersection that creates a trine;
or with one wide chord a well ranged choir
collected its separate throats' desires,
a bolder brew by bringing in its brines.
The basal petals will help you weave
the counterpoint all melodies deserve;
illuminate the marsh lights with your seave,
depict the bend that deepens to a curve,
attend early funerals and learn to grieve,
restrict your thought to acquire reserve.
Review your work. Foretell the vanished verve,
receding creeds you no longer can believe;
note analogies that lose their nerve
in later verse, the margined word the lines won't reeve,
servants searching for another master to serve,
unused steps that watch the mill wheel leave
the still real pond, its slats refine
the horizon by lifting it from a fabler to a liar,
then dive with a figure that requires
the cartwheeled juggler to sweep intestines
in depths where swims the radical marine
to be struggled through a destiny by an apical lyre.
Powering the disks that face the muddy sapphires,
it wanders like a loom or a quadruped's spine.

KICKING THE HORSE

Heroin's dieseled foot pounds locomotive me,
afternoon in the round house, the ceiling's cobs'
and flies' duets in the nets, spruce resin gobs,
spikes distilling rust bled to the votive scree.

I am the sun's core, Phaeton in the garage,
behind each door a journey bums its map.
Reins mangled, shoes thrown off hooves, but parge
white boots for my fetlocks, and grab your subway strap.

Zinc in the sparkler, fire's popsicle,
tides one way its loquacious fuse.
I drive my restive team with a drayer's whistle
to hear the continent's bulletins and the news

from beach detritus, sand's undulant curb
and the epistles in the surf's cursive blurb.

THE HEADBOARD

I

is the transom completing the box,
notched into something postal for shipping
unspoiling freight bumped over long distances,
even the voyage of the night which stops
at the gaudy pigments of the dawn.

An unremediating light intrudes,
polychrome trollop, repainting murals,
stealing the blue's unfulfilled promise,
diluting its blacks, leaving the bituminous
street to shine alone, a mirror homesick
for its nocturnal. Stars are tipped jacks

palmed in between. I am the agony
of indigo, squid's ink's deliquescence,
shuffled in a spectrum, ungathered oil
afraid of its own palette. I stand
in an arbor of violets, nothing prepared,
cringing at the roll call of colors.

II

Saw her in the bathroom's steamed mirror
her pubic triangle's hair without a dick
was complete and involucrate. A hand
swept down would meet no nasty protuberance
only a trim abdomen continued into longing.

The bathrobe was what I would hurry into,
night putting on a blue dawn, the airport's
blue lights snuffed by a mantling. Abandon
the rainy shower curtain its coral folds
showing, the wayward soap an obelisk
of desire floating in the tap spat water,

the avocado oil rinsing each instant
into a sheen, the tangled drain.
The bathmat catches my drips and muffles
feet shortened into girlhood,
the towel despairing of the longer hair,
my lips untightened for a kiss.

III

What if I, stoveblack, cauldron noir,
cul de sac, Styx digs, lose myself,
am diluted? I am an earth under too much
color. What must I give to quarry
the light? Veins of gold and opaque gems,

brooches yearning for their clasps,
asps' backs, the tessellated tortoise,
both conductors that can carry gilt
to and fro. Someone to watch night
strike its evening tents, derubicund
the dusk, darken the leaves into umbrage,

pay the birds to lullaby, phosphor
the woods, shell venus, dull hopscotch
boxes, let down the dew, blackboard
the comets, refresh the stars, background
for neon, firework shooting stars,
and draw lovers closer as a chill sets in.

CHANGE OF DIET

I behave at borders. Something happens
when two areas meet. Diphthongs
recognize this in their double betrayals.
Sand and water elide at all hours.
The future is too close to the present.
All these sleek confederacies are just
a guise for change. I like hiatus, and lines.
When I see light slur right next to shadows,
the mixing disgusts me.
Put me back on solids: Euclid's.

THE AMPHIBIAN

Chequered gecko who kings himself in water,
    whose land tail counterweights, id to my superego,
    croc's clock weight, balancing pole. Tight roped
feet salamander the meandering shore line, waiter

among the spume cloths, ticking bellboy gator
    peterpaning pendulum ambulatory ego
    shifting line of battle cloud front crowd rope
psychomachia's umpire mixing foul and fair.

A tessellated armor glints suits along the seance
    of your spine. Lagoons rinse your bright
tarot, your dragooned galaxy. Infant
    from the sea who trespasses ouija night,
guide me to the dives and digs, let border dance
    loose my feet and neon's venom Venice my canals.

MY CELLAR ANIMAL

My cellar animal is loose again, rubbing
its smooth coat against the cool of the stones,
smelling the circle where the water was bubbling,
laying its tongue on long ice to draw its tone.
I sniff its scent lifting through the hatchway
from the befouled cobblestones of the earth stopped wall.
It stumbles against the joists to have its way
with the house shaking like hay with rats in the fall.
From high mountain grass I run back breathless
to find it still pumping dark measures in my chest.
It bobs as if in water, slicks my tongue, tress-
passes, a slug in cabbage, dark god in guise as guest.
Now you've left me whom you half-conquered
I try to reel the words back in;
I hadn't fed you, had broken concord,
I'd put you up like garden spoil on shelves.
You stand outside the mirror to beckon
with gesture, mime and Gorgon selves.
I'll put your statue half down in flowers,
and play a fountain through your lips.
Snakes will slide away the hours
against the marble of your hips.
And I'll smell mold and rind and root,
gaze down holes and let birth, gravity,
tides and drains pull me mute
until the sun tips the balance with golden audacity.
But you'll be my bedfellow and together will creep
to the bottom of burrows through the soft leaves of sleep.

THE WELL

The well has worn the bent bricks smooth.
Raising low waters on the rungless ladder
which leaves the brim as tongueless adders
to lisp into the beds they soothe.
It has for signposts its lips' worn grooves.
Yet this buried wellhead's ceaseless chatter
is muffled, and I lose the matter,
missing out on palatals and their moods.

I could move closer to the font,
with picks remove the earth from overhead,
as in a lecture I move up front
to hear the slips, and words just barely said;
but I've found stones whose sides will hunt
a crowning circle that will lift the top instead.

THE BUILDER

The whelk's broken chamber keeps a flight
still vaguely turning to a centering goal,
the relic reminding me that it once was whole
by lifting to circles now far beyond its might.

From warm ribs I divine the severed curves
and lull the space with cream and slope of curls,
until my mind eddies, its senses collapse and swirl
in a luxury of coral, around a coral swerve.

The shell uncoiled can strike with leaner nerve.
The venom of its tubes transfixed my stare.
My temples pulsed, the marine creature's verve
crept toward my heart and pulled my feelings bare.
I became the animal once again to serve
with winding steps a diagram of stairs.

THE TRANSFORMATION

The bleached ocean trolls a pale lipped shell,
tuned to a scale in a major key
to quench disorders of the mind, and to quell
the brain hunted down by some thorned melody.

Pulled by storms from the cobbled floor,
with rose flushed out, and collision with shoals
delaying your dizzy animal from reaching shore,
you slide off the silver sea, a weathered water bole.

Trapped by breakers, tracked on the crumbling sands,
the fumbled pool drools your luster and drains
all inner sheen. Sheer riffs of song command
unruly tubes, and golden tones of pipes reclaim

you, forlorn, untamed, broken, wild conch and worn.
Blow notes low and thick from your jazz horn.

THE MUSCLED WHELK CONTRACTS WITHIN THE BRAIN

The muscled whelk contracts within the brain
the unnumbered motions its marbled limb unbends.
The attitude of a recumbent god commends
its grace to rise beyond our ken and train
upon untraveled realms to inhabitants of the frenzied fanes
and the guardians of the wild. A rippling in the posture sends
the startled image through ancient space to when
on pediments the cornered goddesses curled. And the sense cranes
to follow how from that river the limber goddess climbs
to swell upon the temple, resplendent and revealed.
How by pulling on the idle rope to ring the chimes,
and hope to draw devotioners in by music peeled;
And yet how the temple in one stray glance
tempts the river to disrobe and the goddess dance.

AROUND THE DERELICTION OF
THE ACCOMPLISHED WHELKS

Around the dereliction of the accomplished whelks
their whorls strained by the stranding tides, shuffle
the shell pickers, stooping for a conch with milks
and rose blushed, stained by seaweed and muffled

with sand. The sacks of the raiders bulge with plunder,
forms the sea flushed: plush pearls, hued crusts,
swank sets of snails threshed by combers from the thunder-
ing surf. Drunk on lush furled shapes, and dank with lust,

they swagger home with staggering loads to barter in the square,
the porters of the scheduled swells. The wrecks and hurled husks,
dooms in a late pool, the lean gatherer gleans, fair
wan shucks, flanges, flares; moved more by murk than musk,
steered by his quest to strains the broken corals dare,
he reaps their violent postures and travels in the dusk.

THE SPRAYER

Had a place for one but never put one in
until the plumber was going to make some
repairs including reversing the hot and
cold taps. Now its synthetic sleeve topped
with the proud nozzle after spraying
retracts into its socket swaying a bit,
almost undulating to prolong its wet exit
before it bangs on a pot stored underneath,
reminding me of the late May evening when
I was in my college's garden, bent down
and by mistake touched a ground snail
thicker than my thumb, glistening with
a lubricant for its private hole into which
it slunk, hypnotic flesh bidding me adieux.

THE CHESSMEN

So far all haven't surfaced, bobbing
below the Baltic main carved from ice,
loggerheads, marble green bergs
sluicing the arctic sea through their baleen.
The buoy rooks mark a demesne
of white caps with cold cornerstones
that the poleaxed bishops could transfix,
the legless centaurs could crawl american
and the pawns could broker if only the king
and queen could become buoyant,
if only the squares could pane,
if only the whites could double
into the shadow army to start the game.

THE SCAPHANDER

When they come in the middle of the night,
your household sleeping, rain shielding
their footpads, unzipping your screens
with a box cutter or stanley knife to hoist
themselves through a window you turn
in your underworld while they rifle the sewing
cabinet mistaking it for a desk, its spools
confusing them with two a.m. threads,
the pin cushion sea urchining them,
shears stalking their fingers, tape
measuring their intensions, the hemming
chalk marking thieves' low water,
darning needles after some blood,
darning eggs, unavoided ovoids, drunk
from blunt fumbling rocking under their thumbs,
childhood's tops that cannot be stilled,
patterns rustling with money's silkiness
filched screed rustled into bags, the dummy
torso's silence a museum's or garden's,
teller camera, shoulder muse, diving bell alert
for the draper's cloth, the photographer's
hood, Houdini's cloak, then they catch
the sewing machine's treadle and the bobbin
hums, the cloth bunched up behind the stitch,
time waiting to unfold onstage, waiting
for the cannon ball chained to his small lithe
frame to be shucked with the manacles
and cuffs, while mum is the word in your
house, the argot of heists pantomime
silhouette and daguerreotype, so hold
your breath and only exhale at the end
of dreams, it is the hiatus they deserve.

THE SABBATICAL

For days I've wanted to burn my verse
hurl notebooks diagonally into the flames,
or better to have ignited it as it came
fire following with its lavish cursive.

I am leaving. Paper bags stir
behind me. Outside, the wheelbarrow's frame.
Waste paper lit outdoors changes names
against a screen that was the chimney's first.

To keep the animal out and the ashes in,
the carbon of his pelt, the gait of soot
flapping in each other's skin.
Each night the stalking pad put
on my lintel its charcoal rustling, the din
of moths, emissaries from dark's deep glut.

ANGER

The stream can hold more furious speech
than its dry borders show, so seldom filled.
A voice grown from several waters spilled
has heaps of rounded boulders now in reach.

All the tributaries in my maddened brain
collect to bend their voices over stone
which now submerged I can no longer train.
A roar ensues when I would want a tone.

Born upstream that makes of boulders tongues
I'm never warned of flood until I'm reeling.
The rhetoric of anger cannot be sung
in a choir swollen past all feeling.

You are too good a friend. I want a seep
from meadows, not a torrent I can't keep.

THE ASYLUM

Misled by the darkness of the woods,
the after-midnight quiet in the halls,
the old doctor who did all she could,
the grounds where large trees sprawled,
into thinking I was climbing to a room
that held a restfulness that was all mine,
I saw the bedsteads loom
of more than fifty sleepers all in line.
But still hoping that beyond them lay
the separate sanctums for those like me
I followed until I heard her say
This is where your bed will be.
She answered my protest with just these words:
They won't touch you–there are nurses in the wards.

LETTER FROM THE ASYLUM

For a while I balanced on a chessboard.
I saw no need for the pieces
since each square inhabited itself,
full of position and import.
Black and red blinked on and off,
light switches at either end of our den,
the electronics kits Pete built.
I was rank and file and ran up the rows,
a blossom carrying the fire for my Olympics,
scarring the board with wax.
I watched the haughty reds
rein in the jealous licorices
shifting like a sea to spill its tips
into the please of red.
I set my warm soles on the black basalt
and hopscotched, marking my way with chalk.
Parquetry found in our church's basement,
underworld covered over by renovation,
burned with the curious walks of childhood,
the brown diagonals zigzagging with games
made from threes, the shared floor, cornered,
but turning with design.
This was our marble's promenade,
the straightened whistle,
the inlaid box sprung with our grandfather's toys,
the extra lengths the eaves' hardwood
traveled under the cedar chest,
full of army wool over a game of mothballs,
and extra insignia chevronned, promotable.
I placed blocks that looked like colored silos
and north poled the board.
This floe thawed in the channel
and I saw the queen's basements,
porous as combs and the rook
pumping them level, his sucker shoulders
now screwed with hoses, a hydrant at last.

FIELDWORK

They came visiting like glaciers, staying
longer than expected, their long dresses
eskers compacting the hallways. They perched

on the ends of beds like hanging valleys, and queried
us with pool deep blue eyes, small talking
until we babbled in return. Into the plain

of the men's ward they flowed, stepping from inmate
to inmate, as if they were crossing a stream
on flat rocks. It could have been wartime, but most

there had no brides, few visitors except what
the medicine couldn't block, free riders in an aisle
of screams. The room seemed warmer as old

social skills revived; smiles stretched to meet
mouths happy at college. Then they began
to melt, retreating almost with curtsies

to a polite distance around their supervisor,
while one by one we fell out of love.

THE VISITORS

Those of you who've never been in wards
in a county where the roads are strange
might not know the words
with which the student nurses come
greeted at the door by unusual inmates.

They divide the room in portions with their skirts
to learn the firmness of selected beds,
while beside each one the subject flirts
as she tries the queerness of his head.

I knew of nurses from my work,
had even supervised my share,
now could study all my quirks
since I'd been shaved and had combed my hair.

Yet I lacked the grin that could beguile
a moment's mate that once a month
passed the watch house and the stile
to play the therapeutic hunch.

So you must imagine on your own,
the conversations they employed,
what gentle speech in gentler tones
by other patients was enjoyed.

MANIA

My lightning needs a world to land on,
rattles its bolts in the umbrella stand.
I stir my soup with gravity's hand,
for even that whirlpool mounts in wild abandon

like math behind a fraction.
Everything has a rotational momentum.
Thrown pots swell to their farthest rands.
A broken whelk is strung with axioms.
Suns queue. I flock to a grove, land,
let down my roots, windy cables,
and feed to a color from fathoms.

Guy wires on my transmitter thrash.
My tower shrieks with night
stations stars morse in dot and dash.
Words chord, charge a flight
to match the speed of a telegraph
arpeggioing darkness into light.

RISPERDAL

I am in the middle of May.
The groundskeeper's lights are all to the fore,
throwing an arrogance of runway flares
down the surprised grass and into the clumps of bushes.
The road is a pink orange independent of dawn.
Vines rood here and the stars would genuflect,
but already an undulant blue, an incense drifting in,
is beating back vespers that held out for so long.

THE MAGNETO

and lead us not into temptation but deliver us
from evil if you know the good you will do it
I know the good but I cannot make myself do it

on the ward I thrash in nightmare's sheets
the nurse dumbstruck at my vile mouth
a drummer piping wildly on his fife

I pitch a frantic hay to the witch's stall
life burns with a fuse for a wick
I Amsterdam my tricks on every street

stars accumulate on my looking glass
the turning barber pole Mays its ribbons
the autumn wind unsexs the milkweed's pods

volcanoes clink their slag in firepink troughs
words are buoyant are buoys in my tide
I match the colossus in its stride

I leave the doctor trailing in my wake
or sounding the depths as I grind to shore
he kedges my ship as it shifts its ballast

or tugs me from an empire's worth of sand
the lifeline's clip slides rapid as a chain
each link I cinch counts against my gain

THE RENAISSANCE MAN

I am not angry if I'm not well rounded.
Eclectic archer with a quiver of skills,
in my full fathomed nursery I sounded

out the octopus, eel, fell mantas and confounded
a Dalmatian, changing the spots on its quilt.
I am not angry if I'm not well rounded.

I kept my high school coach astounded
playing with my bagpipes without a kilt.
In my full fathomed nursery I sounded

the fitness of my mother's breasts, hounded
her nipples, sweet lozenges that didn't melt.
I am not angry if I'm not well rounded,

polymath, athlete, warmed dough well pounded,
volleyer, skater, sword up to the hilt.
In my full fathomed nursery I sounded

my mother's dicta, unsolvable menus, grounded
myself to teams, and smiled through silt.
In my full fathomed nursery I sounded
I am not angry if I'm not well rounded.

THE CATHERINE WHEEL

Going up to the camp attic for no good reason
Dad found a pinwheel on a board
and nailed it to a tree. The tube snaked hideously
and I ran into the pines as he brought

a match to its tail, fearing another one of his explosions,
but from behind all was smoke, the powder trail of a meteor,
the Ostrogoth's' hubs screeching across

Rome's pavements, a brand burrowing deeper into an animal,
a flame turning in its groove, a childhood resurrected under torture.
Oh come see, my mother called,

to stare transfixed stupidly into the face of a new gorgon crucified
on my shield.

THE WATER HOUSE

Bricks climb a spine of mortar
from side to side, pause to curb a window,
stop in a line at the eaves overhanging
a pond pulled by a gang of gears.

At evening this rook wades
and drinks, dunks a course of
masonry level with a stilled
armory of blades. Cattails and goose quills

stir against a basement therapy waits to expose.
On a grounds pass in the spruces
I take an extra breath.
At the other end through the lilies
goldfish poured out of glass
bowls swim from childhoods forced to adult hobbies.

From the hospital above, I will be
dumped to where I started.

One of us, her mouth a gill
in air, taunts those who tied her,
ready to unknot submerged, an acrobatic
for the water house.

The father strands, the mother devours.

TAKING STOCK

Two goldfish dumped in a glass bowl one
for each twin swim the short circuit
or cross the center in a truant
radius. We cannot tell them apart but name
them anyway. We do not drop too much food
but watch them moueing in the lukewarm
water rise to each wet crumb.
When we change it, we put them
in a lock until the level's risen. Dad
set a castle inside nothing but arches so
we see each glide in and out of the
cemented columns. They're matches we throw
flaring in the close air of the incinerator,
or ducats lost in a sandy bottom
or a sunset after the perfect punishment.
We do not cover them at night like birds
but let them pull the twilight round the rim.
We take them to the hospital pond
up the winding driveway too curved for
ambulances where we tip them into
the privacy of reedy water.

GROWTH

The elevation of leaves driven to the attic.
bobbing waist high, the equator of apples,
round and brown in the burgeoning brook.

The wayward scythes divide the wheat in half.
Summer comes around like bloom on fruits,
whose dawn rolls in as shell blush.

My raveling parings the snake's valet sloughs.
The gourd's spur has goaded to its seeds.
Circle me with force. Break me riding to a sweat.

SAN MINIATO AL MONTE

Overlooking Florence this 11th century church
repeats the black and white layered marble facade
found in churches at its foot. Composite,
rectangular mints. A mask had been following me
for days, a mother in an old nightmare. And now,
looking down at the end of a shallow trough,
a drain, facesize, with four almond eyes
tilted to each corner, looks up. "I see you've arrived."
I can hardly disorganize this mask back
to its function. Inside inlaid on the floor,
via the trade routes and crusades, Byzantium
has visited and left its motifs on seven huge
quadrangles leading to a raised choir,
which the crypt heaves up with capitals
exposed to me in the nave. The drains's
four eyes now switched to a squared
tile, dove toward the center at a fifth.
In a cross that cut a circle into fourths
I could feel it pulsing, chafing, aching
to throw off this guise and do me damage.
I walked on a gravel path among cypresses
oozing pee honey resin and around a hedged
garden. I tried the gate and inside picked
a golden globe from a leafless tree of fruit,
one that Eris rolled into Thetis' wedding.
The stem broke like a birth cord.

THE THERAPIST

The gust in your hand wrecks my tree's leaves
whose long black limbs are trembling into sight.
My tears well up like buds from heavy rains.

Ordering me to renew unspeakable grief,
you bring my hidden cares around to light.
The gust in your hand wrecks my tree's leaves

The aspects of your face move me as verbs.
In nakedness and clarity is your delight:
My tears well up like buds from heavy rains.

You slip from robes and I immediately revoke
before your larger power my plan for flight.
The gust in your hand wrecks my tree's leaves.

Your eyes collect me when I look away,
and convey me rattling through my fright.
My tears well up like buds from heavy rains.

Dancer among the lunatics you reveal
yourself behind your trappings and your might.
The gust in your hand wrecks my tree's leaves.
My tears well up like buds from heavy rains.

PSYCHOTHERAPY

My horizon sick at heart swallowed the moon
in a glass of night. An unwitnessed medicinal.
A doctor was the leader of my journey.
He sat in the chair in my bedroom
and laid bare the injuries to my soul.

My anger flocked like a pack of cards
whose crow suits, grounded on the runaway,
were clocks undeployed to belfries.
Handless I ticked an unnumeraled hour.
I heard an octave shouting in my chest.

I was a hydrant octopussed with hoses
no baton could conduct, no key could score,
a spectrum choking on a rainbow,
a hurt curtain of rain waiting
for wind, a storm of lines my mouth

had closed around, telephone poles
counted across a continent on hold, on hold.
Protean so that I could lose him,
I feinted and feigned in a maze
of tropes, but always in my rearview

mirror he followed headlong, lights on,
in the sinuous curves my Lernean highways
writhed, even making the ferry as the last chain
dropped, Charon pacing the deck with me
along the handrail the black lake plunged beneath,

breathing the diesel on the observation platform,
releasing the solitary gulls above the shale
and cedar islands, letting me go public or private
as I finally rejoiced in all I had stored
the unsifted ore of my unbroached thesaurus.

THE PATIENT

To the one who has been made well, again
is whole, even the flowers are calmer in
their growth. The frenzy in his veins has been
freed, and steady blood his usual heart sends.
He who in his hours my slow soul would mend,
leaning or rocking through my thick and thin,
explored with me the memories of the kin
that framed my outlook and hedged me then.

I lent him words that later I took back,
formed now my two mouths they had shared a tone
as will a pool's newer water which slacks
the shape the earlier knew alone,
or rattling trees standing back-to-back
trading spaces with branches whose leaves have flown.

THE EAGLE

I

A capstan winches you, undulant
over mountains new shadows summarize,
each link ratcheted chisels histories
stored in a reservoir against your tyrant.

Whose house is this that flies so gold a pennant
that the sun dims and the stars stay netherwise?
The oceans still to capture such surprise.
The forest's coat, as if from spring, turns vibrant.

Wind master dragged by an iron tail,
you strain against the anchor's groin,
slacken then tighten as you put on all sail.
In what mint will your fettered coin
be dropped, your brilliant feathers to flail
dead air, failed wings too weak to join?

THE DREAM
II

In the dungeon your feathers gleamed like scales.
Your wings dragged, your talons could not fend
off despair, sheathed in a scabbard that portended
the bright promise of your molting mail.

You dreamed that an evening paled
over a mountain, blue and black blended,
the unrehearsed stars rose, their lights pent
overhead and way off wind wailed.

Then Cygnus reaching tip to tip, white fires aloft,
bloomed, burning a journey air
could never hold, black wings that never tire
gliding with multitudes of confreres,
and looked kindly as if he were your sire,
bringing in his train none fleeter if more fair.

THE RETURN
III

Your trammel chafed and woke you. Beside
you was a forge, whose coals numerous as the stars,
brought the dream back. You plunged your leg far
enough to brighten the ring, worked the bellows, tied

the chain to the anvil, hammered and pried,
then broke the manacle with a crowbar.
You kicked the chain free and through the hangar
sparks shot and the din was pent inside.

You shoved a door then running leapt and scooped
the air under your wings, leaving grass and trees
and the treasury where you'd been cooped,
the zephyrs and the paper stirring breeze
for gusts, wind and storm's thunder, and whooped
at usual things, all new, now you were free.

THE CUSTOMER IS ALWAYS RIGHT

The wooden doors with their incised panels
shut my father in the den he used as an office.
He levers slides of monuments
onto the projector screen.

The bereaved do not see the slides but pictures
of their lost one click with each change:
bundled up for winter on the front porch
or carrying a bucket through a verge of maples.

Dad's deep voice is the most distinct.
He hands his clients granite samples.
Cool, polished, heavy feldspar, quartz
and unknown greens clack with each return.

The Cold Spring Granite Company
has done its best, but they turn
and say what do you think,
which one would be right for us.

ASTRONOMY LESSON

My mother was one of Zeus's moons
at the end of my telescope, circling,
with the precision of distance,
the almost indomitable body of my father.
Hera was not chaste but she couldn't condone
his salesman's flings winked in daylight,
a progeny of smiles and pouts,
a mouth narrowed by genetics,
so cute to kiss. Summer was his fair circuit,
the monuments winched down in crates,
potted cedars cutting in, your name here,
typos graven or something to be matched
with names in a family bible, rectory,
or baby's book. A tabula rasa waiting for
a tardy star to fall. Pre need.
I'd watch the display for him—
mostly older people, hand out cards
or take down names and phones,
a shady register for my father.
My mother was not one for cemeteries.
She did not drive or clean, but cooked,
listened to opera and read Faulkner.
She could have been from Dixie.
She's gone now. South.

THE PLEIADES

In the eave's closet with its slanted door
that sloped into its triangular corner,
a quiver of clubs slept with bags of tees
and balls. Although sciatica kept my father

off the green, he was no astronomer.
In our family the stars had to wait for me.
I would lie down with him and my brother
to demonstrate the isosceles

of Deneb, Vega and Altair. I flushed
meteors, corralled planets, whetted
the moon. An owl hooted. We hushed.
Its mate higher in the glen from fretted

branches answered. I led them down,
Cassiopeia, Perseus, Pleiades, Hyades,
Orion, and Sirius. They said Aldebaran
after me. Seers, heroes, and dryads

rose above the mountains. The ink
of unwritten skies. The turning brink.

THE PERSEIDS

We lined up our chaise lounges like wharves
pointing to the harbor of the shooting stars
despite a waning moon that could rise to mar
the annual August pomp, and clouds' grey scarves.

Coyotes echoed owls, warm breezes uncovered
the summer triangle: Deneb in Cygnus, Lyra's
Vega, Altair winking past a conifer far
above the brook and the field unharvested.

North to South swept glowing heads and trails
unpredictable as joys and sorrows.
Soon like phosphors they would fail
their memory fading into tomorrow.
Yet as on a photographic plate the fulgent tail
etched its path and a mane of the whitest yellow.

I AM A STAR WITHOUT ASTRONOMERS

I am a star without astronomers.
White fire that no scope or glass has caught
burns in the solitude that heaven prefers.

All stars' fraternity I abjure
rising apart from those that evening brought.
I am a star without astronomers.

Scan woods, you won't see me above a conifer
where gems breathe spectrums. What I've got
burns in the solitude that heaven prefers.

No almagest records me or footnote obscures
my majesty with what the pedants taught.
I am a star without astronomers.

I elude constellations. Groups in meadows defer
my sighting for a clearer sky. What they sought
burns in the solitude that heaven prefers.

But if alone you summon me, undeterred
by space and time, I'll brighten in my plot.
I am a star without astronomers
that burns in the solitude heaven prefers.

THE WATERFALL

An apple tree in its longevity
more stippled than any colander,
in fruitless arcs sprays its limbs to leaves,
bends to the brook a weary calendar.
An isthmus of gravel sorted to size
fades to black dirt, charcoal pulverized
drawn off poplar filled fields, broken glass,
and small triangles from plates someone passed,
or alone, served it where it was cooked
in a house above, whose cellars tip to grass
beside the ranges its windows overlooked.

A rapid over clumped stones in no key
draining the color from early October,
sizzled from a shallow pool, effortlessly
whitening the channel between two boulders.
My nephew, my brother and I summarize
my father, his father and uncle who surprised
speckled rearranging in pools shadows last
seen slitting open the gravel belly's sack.
Don't think cousins too in the twenties didn't spook
toads by boulders' hips, catch crayfish, track
salamanders to their muddy dens and hook

dreams rootless as wishes at thirteen. I see Mary,
my father's sister, untimely taken, her shoulders
huddled in a coat, the wind, no longer wary
of anything, bending the yellowing November
meadows where she walked with dad, rise upon rise
in blueberry season, harebells in their bluest guise,
and shied the bear and climbed the boulder. No lack
of open space then. Orchards and stone walls backed
up to the kilns, domed hives the frost shook
to the ground, bricks in circles ice shackled.
Showering their cones ahead of them, dark rooks

marshal their wide groves floored with needles, ferry,
shadowing the slopes, the penitential conifers
descending as a bannister, in apses and ambulatories
cloaking the streams again, shaking their boughs over December.
Only from photographs can we surmise
the tepid water of the uncanopied stream. Guy
wired weeds then as now looped by black
pools, and milkweed unzipped fat sacks,
plump registers of seeds undreamed in pillows. The brook
bulged by sunk boulders, split at islands, lost track
in sands, regathered, bringing currents to every nook,

balancing dragon flies above its silver carry.
Its frugal currents have made us closer.
Around a summer waterfall we often tarry,
scout flat stones to lay between two boulders,
shovel in gravel as the pool, unsatisfied,
seeks an outlet we never realized.
Below we're deepening the channel, pack
stone into the sides, scoop out the pool, rack
rock on rock above to raise the dam and look,
the pool has wet the lip where it will pass,
and spill to the waiting pool below. We took

the height of the waterfall and stacked
another foot on top. Let our father stay intact
by the same measure, filling and entering. In the crook
we can't see around, water bugs skip like jacks.
Wrinkles in the apple tree overlook this brood.

HOMUNCULUS

Parish god I rolled you out of stream clay
    peppered with gravel too rough for glaze,
    left you to dry on the sill until in stove ash
I dropped you to harden for a day.

Each time I stoked it you were in the way
    so I moved you with the tongs to outlast
    the maple and the coals it cast.
I put you on your knees so you could pray.

I need no cones to tell when you've been fired
    as if they teach in Hades by degrees.
The look I want is when all hope's expired,
    scorified by smoke's incendiaries,
a tabula rasa, a landlord absentee
I'll pinch from the stove to worship me.

THE RECUPERATION

the sky is an invalid tonguing a yellow lozenge
from cheek to cheek that whets strops on a night
of tides coughing a delirium of dreams awake waves
keep from the shore to stop the shell from grinding
on grains of sand fever favorite of the thermometer
to dissolve the moats of the childhood castle
rush a gritty slurry down its avenues salting its larynx
with a caustic gargle a sun caught in Stonehenge's
throat our heart in a barrel of ribs thudding in place
hooves pawing in a stall of straw without a chariot
to tow across the heavens a dawn we never went
to sleep for seeded by the homesick planets
the stars hastening to their constellations
waiting for a second comet to sound its knell

THE COMET

More blurred than early photography, you pass
in the eastern sky, the caliph's wheelhouse,
first observable beneath Arcturus.
Too rare for anything but disaster,

Taiwan may well shudder as stock crashes
on the mainland at unification's hour.
Already Orwelled by Belfast, London's bourse
would not welcome you, cold fire at Easter.

But you're a runner beyond the crowd's cheers.
Indifferent to hope and despair, only by
coincidence do our sad affairs in arrears
astrologize your return, the once barren sky
uncanny again from your arctic career,
snowball from the walls of the other side.

DIVESTITURE

The sun's foreclosing November,
a dark fire, burning out on the hearth.
The lilacs' leaves the final plunder
the wind corners on the porch.

The sunset's just a bar of gold chased
with a flagon of gray I drink to the lees.
Geese picking at the furrow's waste
will be a chain straightened in the skies.

I am an instrument of my father
asked to a grave in his father's town.
The line I scrawl will pen my own death.
I look for a field where I can settle down.

The ditch's water glistens. It repays
interestingly enough the final rays.

TRANSFORMATIONS

Daffodils take the opposite route of finches
whose male in the midst of the third march storm
cannot help himself but across his shoulder inches
a patch of yellow the first in a flock for seeds

descending to the ground beneath my feeder,
while in a glass vase cut gray-green stalks warm
to buds that break so flavously form
a cup and blow petals not found in weeds.

False paper blossoms dim to orange from yellow
astounding even Midas with their glut of gold.
Soon a torch of almost jonquil
will brighten head, wing and breast,
nights will shorten, warmth swap cold
until the sun retreats to rest.

AFTER THE HARVEST

My scarecrow hands are mute and expostulatory,
knuckles are red from the cold, a glove of gasoline.
The crows that paint the cornfield waver
above my outstretched arms and mosaic smile.
A vane, I turn in a gust of wind, direct
another set of furrows. The stirred clouds'
pigments sizzle round the lightning's splinter,
lap the blonde stick wading in their center.
The crows widen their circle priming its borders
with a coat of black. Rough soil stubbled with
cracked shale and glacial till glints flint shards
rained from a clay bed. The clouds brush the horizon
black and gray closing the white off from the south,
penning me in a cell of fallen light, the sun broken
into corn husks trashed amid the stalks. The wind
mines the rising moon ain'ting in the clouds,
a sulk of yellow drawn in childhood, miming
with the eloquence of her curve the dolors of growth.
A few stars crocus, then the vast Pacific of the sky,
and a star scythe to cut down my starched form
and let me breathe and run.

TRANSUBSTANTIATION

swept a broom down to its knub no longer
good for corners but kept it anyway
time for a new one which I leaned on the porch
along with the hoe if the drain clogged
my spud for ice the cultivator for the garden
snow shovel rake pitchfork we played pick up sticks
with my grandfather's game of tiny wooden
tools dropping a handful of implements
on the table and then picking until the pile
shifted lining up our captures in front
one day I reached for it and it was gone
but all the other tools were there
straw went into a nest somewhere
maybe even the shelf to the right of my door
which a robin used to witch her young
out of the nest to a west of their own

AUTUMN AT CAMP

The candle long from the mold stands in its holder
its wick sculpts through drifts of wax
carried in its sconce to snuff night's darks
and burn a light that only makes us older

the wind pries against the attic shutters
blows rhomboid leaves across the fall green lawn
each animal is packing deep its burrows
with cone seed and nut from dusk to dawn

each pool turns a carousel of leaves
a kaleidoscope that fits its jagged puzzles
the silver white falls slip carefully away
with a glistening neck to the basin just below

moss on boulder flowers between the stones
remind me that I'll never be alone

NEW MINTAGE

sluiced from the ground in a late autumn rain
effluvium of the downspout's small flood
the gutter gathered the roof released
unprospected yet panned I held it under
a faucet to rinse the mud off not a cement
dollop coin round igneous sparkles light catches
a little wider and thicker than a silver dollar
mica quartz I thought friable at first but not
even frangible a cracker I can't break unlike
the soda top he would pinch between his
thumb and finger until its teeth clenched
then hand it over to me while I struggled
to buckle mine my young grocer's face red
with the strain

LETHE

Coiled in the top drawer of my father's bureau was a score
of belts, the tongue tucked inside its buckle clinked outside
a nest of snakes without a hiss sleeping the winter in Florida
leather, plastic, fabric, skin, rope, jute, metal, you can wear
only one belt at a time. It looked like a store. No one keeps
the clothing of the deceased. My grandfather didn't want to
see another woman walking around town in his wife's dress
so when she died he had them burned. Furniture is handed
down, collections, papers, keepsakes, mementoes, a pillbox
of silver, an old man with a hunchback of matches, a wooden
urn turned on a lathe. A glass case of fossils and minerals my
great grandfather and great uncle combined, a sideboard that
was a doctor's payment, the retort, cash books, vials and tubes
almost enough to pharmacy with. And my dad's razor whose
top I sprung open to find his last whiskers which I blew into
the wastebasket as I would my own.

NO QUARTER

We had a regimen by which we banned
death's subtle columns from our father's limbs.
We marched in love then let it have its whim
and turned the wheelchairs into cannon.

On the sentried parapets we outmanned
its siege with embrasures fit with medicines,
let our sleep's wick be trimmed
by his, our hands at best like his hands.

Still, death sounded the mortar of the walls,
fire in a trench or an ambuscade,
and soon his minions in the halls
were a rabble we would not stay,
water in his quarters, pale beyond recall,
to float his soul for winds no earth has made.

CARRION

Family come first to pick the flesh, pecking
into cupboards and chests, pards in the library,
footing the altitudes of the stacks to shake
each book for money. They fan the passbooks
pigeon holed in the desk. They stir drawers,
puddling the indexes of years, reopen letters,
sending a thick thumb down creases for dollars,
dump files for wills, upsetting the alphabet,
scattering the mosaic of a lifetime underfoot.
Lifting the glass doors of the cabinets they sweep
quartz diamonds into sacks, throwing fossils
and shells aside. They upend the coin jars
and pick out the quarters, pushing the rest
toward the children, folding the stray bills
into their pockets. They load antiques into their
cars, consigning the sideboard and strident
piano to the gavel, call the junk man for the couch
and bookcases, stray furniture too embarrassing
to auction and the book dealer in his truck.
He wheels a dolly onto the porch and looks
for hardbound, first editions, leather, old stuff,
all hopefully unmarked. They want him
to take all of it, but he calls another man
who comes and strips everything readable out,
even the more than fifty notebooks at last count,
that hold the styles of poetry in wavering columns,
the stuff of hearts in keepsakes from the pen.

CHESS AFTER DEATH

Two rooks down their father's aisles
brim to the neglected horizon,
top the cornered ranks with cemetery posts.
The pantheon, now a queen's palindrome,
drowns its roster for our father taken under.
Relatives and friends queue for positions.
Tonight the hectic bishop is an uncle
booed by jealous clerics in their stalls
anxious for my checkered psyche.
The sidelined king crowds to the frozen
pond, the past stolling his shoulders,
and watches the sciamachy of his twin sons.
His thirst pinks to a salt block,
parches in an ice house sawdust mortars.
Black's reflections pose in the channels
of concentric squares a weighty alarm.
My brother dismantles me
with an unmatchable paradigm.
My almost molten goldfish
congeal from their fluid selves,
and I am Narcissus over ice
locked from my supple other.
Yet from a well found in its castle
the hydrant floods the board,
and we skate regardless of squares
into the warming house
where dad sleeps by the stove.

FIREFLIES

Phosphors lessened under the duress of twilight
still blink a dirge for the sidewise fallen rabbit
hit and run and the wet imprint his body made
a shadow no sun could cast a dismal urine bath.
Stars brightened in the pan of developing night
synced too and the rumbling trucks' headlights
tapped harmonic morse among the tree's distant
branches so full of summer leaves each autumn
strips. I gently prodded the body into the weeds
and turned it once again to leave it undisturbed.
I don't ask any more for myself when at the end
wound at last in the swaddling clothes of death
I cannot budge the stone against my tomb.

HOLY SATURDAY

On the way to Chatham on Shaker Museum Road
I struck and killed a hedgehog. I am no speeder
but she didn't have a chance on a spring errand
crossing the road from under the pasture's wooden
fence. A swerve but the thump of wheel on bone.
On the way home I passed her already
carrion with a crow standing by her. I doubled
back and pulling off on the shoulder flashers on
rolled her onto the grass so she wouldn't be hit
again. She had eight more breasts than my
grandmother whom I helped out in bed
an unembarassed Methodist unwound from
her sheets saying we're all the same underneath.
I turned around in the driveway of the alpaca
farm whose glut of crocus I guess I'll count as Easter.

REINCARNATION

When I come back it will be as iron:
Firedogs embers firework from,
or a stave that brick strains against
two stories above a granite foundation.

Not even as grass let alone an orange
and black beetle on the top of a limestone
wall undulated by an abandoned
farm's meadow in a late July afternoon.

I will interrupt Vulcan limping to his bellows
hammer and tongs clanging at his hip
to forge for me a renovation. Sparks will blow
an obdurate life into me, and skip
the cells please, I want to rust or glow,
no pith, seed, blood or gills this trip.

BEWILDERED

I stand on the floor of a golden wood
waiting for its leaves to fall. A brook runs
a dry and bouldered course waiting for thunder
and lightning to swell the rains to island

boulders restore old pools plan
ripped side channels for overflow dun
each freshet with tripped soil stun
the salamander crammed in the root ball.

Things will never be the same again. They
never were. Each era a wind drives down
drafts in mountain vales shivering with

the future. The ascent's easy the descent
hard last year's leaves clotting a false path
are those the mountains that will guide us home?

THE DUMP

was just north behind a cedar hedge
on the curving beach of Lake Champlain.
Bathers obscured by its smoke
refreshed themselves in the summer waters.
We drove there when we had something
to dispose of. Their trucks parked
on the discards, alert for copper, tin
and brass, picking scavengers mimicked
the gulls, helped pull trash from our trunks.
The glint of broken bottles thumped
on what must have been sand beneath
mocked with its jagged wave the wind
pushed swells hissing to glassy shores.
The worst of households tumbled,
undulating toward Canada, consigned
to the combined hells of rotting sofas,
quit fridges, unglued furniture.
Its democracy beat the cemeteries'
segregated by sect. I'd like to be
buried among its cans and plastic,
my only monument a gull screeching
over an inland sea.

THE LOCUST TREE

At my grandfather's the clack
of my rake against the seed pods,
some torn along the top like feed bags,
the bitter smell bruised out of them,

the seeds finished until almost slippery.
I never noticed them on the trees
but they branded the yard if you left them,
the lawn taking their photograph.

Dried they rattled when shook
jumping in their private sockets.
I want to leave with one, my fingers
pried open for its long black capsule.
Lost, I'll want Hades to hear me coming.

THE GARTER SNAKE

Coiled in three inches of grass, your head
resting on a loop, I follow each bend
and hiss the consonants of a new

language. Oblivious to the rain,
your patience occult to me, I don't wait
for your glide but turn away reminded

even by your stasis of my inelegant gait.
Poised, oiled, avoirdupois, belly
the color of pollen, head streaked with gold,
was I the treasure you were guarding,
or were you, charnel rattle, hiring out as guide?

THE UNBLAZED TRAIL OF PRAISE

I've never seen the prairie. It must start
soon out of Buffalo, the farthest I've been west,
under whose streets Lake Erie, sharing shores
with Canada, flattens its sheet.

Wagons with furniture rattled west,
and secretaries were set out by the trail
mile after mile.

The night after mom died I opened
a packet of my poems from her desk.
She'd written: "Brilliant" "Sad but beautiful"

There's Ohio but I cannot think what's next.

THE CEMETERY MOWERS

The one wheeled edging hand mower nudges
the unfinished bases of monuments, unpolished
plinths the lengths of grasses spike, dividing
the granite into blue grey star points clippers
will snuff, trimming the wicks of dandelions,
prowling around the corners for shadows.

No blade can stand this scrutiny. Shears
litter the ground with the fallen, raised
from the earth, measured by the sun. Graveled
roads rectangle the plots, corner stoned
and piped off with old iron. Norfolk spruce
ground their boughs in a hedge against the hill.
The larger mowers whir in the distance,
take the easy paths that crosscut lots,
a spray of grass churned by the helical blades
softening each step out of respect for those gone.

ICARUS

If I could fly again, it wouldn't be
in myth, a waxed bat from the labyrinth,
between the breakers and the sun's squint
pushing my quills over the islanded sea,

but on grown wings in the worst century,
my shadow, flattened on the round earth's plinth,
an epitaph for the slain, the prisoner's torment,
a dirge for the cruelties after Normandy:

two gentle flights over the Sea of Japan,
the light that landed from a broken spectrum
stopping the world before it had begun;
the midased corpses, the braid of human
hair, the lamp shades and the almost fecund
boxcars switched to a siding and undone.

ANIMAL CRACKERS

The box, a barred circus cart, encloses
the blonde tang of lions, the giraffe's
domino, the elephant in soft outline.
Elgin metopes quarried out of flour.
Apollo's quadriga set in a deep square
whose top soffits level the horses' heads,
waits as if he had no other dawn by yours.
The frieze's next frame is Perseus slaying
Medusa, one hand holding her head up
which would have lolled on the blade.
They face us, she on one knee.
Finally Hercules bears the Cercopes,
twins on a pole upside down
and symmetrical in their defeat.
Yet their arms are folded and they're
smiling, their feet rest on his shoulders,
and their thighs, even larger than
Hercules', make angles with their calves
that enlarge him further. These twins
were notorious at deception but Hercules
caught them as they buzzed
around his face as blue bottles
and forced them to their native shape.
Upside down they had a great look
at his but which had been burned black
by the sun and the fiery breath
of the Cretan bull. They began to laugh
and when Hercules found out the cause
he sat down and laughed and they persuaded
him to release them. In tarot
le pendu though hung by his left ankle

upside down nonchalant has crossed
his right behind where he's hidden
his hands. And Houdini was never
happier than when submerged manacled
under ice. Odysseus never at a loss.
A trick to everything. Don't look
at the Medusa. The sun can be harnessed,
animals tamed, grain cultivated.
Keep your cool. Keep your head.

RECUMBENT ON THE KNOLL
WHERE BLOWN GRASS IS

Recumbent on the knoll where blown grass is
twining a replica of hands wound in grief
I hear the creak of heaven's axis

Raising like the fruit above the gaunt chassis
of Tantalus stars new tonight as leaves.
Recumbent on the knoll where blown grass is,

I'm met with meteors for Niobe's trespasses
that last as long as her father's pool is brief.
I hear the creak of heaven's axis,

the bulging bow, the seven lasses
falling with lads, unfeathered shafts in each.
Recumbent on the knoll where blown grass is

I hear the brook in its passes
carrying from stone-to-stone tears beyond reach.
I hear the creak of heaven's axis.

scattering stars like a cold fire's ashes
washed up too late on Leto's beach.
Recumbent on the knoll where blown grass is,
I hear the creak of heaven's axis.

MAKING MY BED

I unfolded the map of the pillowcase
and fitted the four corners of the dream world
in, leaving the next resident to trace
their night journey with its cool, white folds.

I unfurled the bottom sheet that knew the way
soothing the mattress with a cotton caress.
The partner top floated and had its say
then waited patiently for the coverlet next.

I would not lie down there again. Bags packed,
I rechecked the bureau's wooden drawers.
I flicked the switch but turned to look back
and wished a hundred nights and even more

to hear the breeze rustle outside the screen
and watch foliage turn from black to green.

LIKE CLOCKWORK

In my brother's basement, the snow's blue
chloroxes the walls. A SAD light
falsifies an early spring on a workbench
strewn with brass pins and gears.

Loyal to the present, the combined movements
of all the clocks cannot advance the vernal
equinox by a second. Even clocks that dabble
with the moon, that jut its quarters in cutouts
on their face, are hapless with the future.

Chained weights drag a day through
its turns, laundry spun and dried,
the sun on rinse again, the color washed
out of a corona too dull to couple.

With double crossing hands, the clocks
trick toward February, an anvil in a pond,
gravity against my brother, hardly closer
to the northern Spring.

The heater chugs at his legs. The magnified
works beam back two century's gold wheeled
in a clock that has not struck in years. Beyond
his pliers circles the zodiac captive in his shop,
a domestic sidereal, but unable to infuse,
in a ticking universe, the brightness he requires.

GENERAL DELIVERY

Where are the family, children and
mother, wife and lover, yarded leaves
under cover of deep snow that drifts sheave,
pouring it back and forth like sand?
What son from me will take command
throwing the old views out to the breeze?
What daughter in that great chain from Eve
will stir lost hearts to search for something grand?

My steps will end in a local wood
just as spring has hedged its borders
and the sky nudged a planet overhead.
My thoughts will share a vine's disorders
as spiraling over weeds it spreads.
Wild animals will be my only warders.

THE PROMPTING

Be still my heart for another heart is beating,
be still my breath another chest does rise.
Cease looking, another has your eyes,
no listening save for what has stopped retreating.
No voice for all syllables are fleeting,
no thought to ambush you in wild surprise.
No touch no smile no smell no taste no cry,
each wound you have another now is healing.

Wings lift to soar above their earth
the domain of sky its sun, moon and stars
celebrate the second of your births.
With each infant's face God has gone so far
to form a look that ends its mother's search.
Call on your divine and the unfamiliar.

THE ACROBATS

Widening their arcs towards windier margins
then their ropes have coasted to for crowds before,
they train them now swaying to their target,

their feet arranging sawdust on the floor.
The somersaults his body will unravel
bulk up like loops that coiled rope stores.

With the consistency of a metronome that travels
the nimble circuit its box constricts, she nicks
the blunt edge of where they'll meet, a gavel

setting stone. The net stretches its web knit
for falls. His full trunk nudges him in time,
and he hoists himself into that void, towards the trick,

now tumbling like a wall, reaching for a rhyme,
a dull ache arching him toward her grasping wrists.
He unbundles from the tuck and grabs her wide arms,
shedding like skins three- and one-half twists,
held safe, almost home, free from all harm.

AMPHITRITE

Out of work and the mental hospital
I got a tan that made people turn. Boy
you look good. But I didn't feel

that good. One Saturday a girlfriend
of my wife's came out to share the heat
of August on our beach. She changed

in the room which was one large bed,
and came out with the curves of frond,
shore and shell. For the first time

on the beach there was seaweed which
went with her as she rose for the water,
and later streamed behind her as she swam.

I spoke with her with the water as interpreter,
leveling our midriffs until our words came out
like breaths. I had spoken with a woman

in Santa Domingo at about the same depth,
and the four of us went out for dinner,
prawns, and riding in a carriage with

each other spouses. However, this woman,
smelling a marriage left to burn on the stove,
left early taking the evening with her.

JAYWALKING

Rail fences like x's in an attendance book
crossed lots groves closed with their borders.
Ranks of corn stalks kept crows at work.

Geese drew closer, then settled in a far field,
and I imagined their cackling in the barren rows.
Barbs hooked at my clothing as I struggled

in a swaying fence, like a long note before
it's bumped from the sax's swelling throat
by a plural following. Ditches claimed me,

miscellaneous moats had me as their guest.
Trespassing in those privileged corridors,
a scarecrow, I startled their dusty tassels,

as I rubbed the weed pods like a brushing wind.
My truancy ended among a crowd of trees,
clumped on a mild slope they seemed to own.

Their branches in a unison of gestures pulled
somber umbrage within their forking crowns.
I raised my arms and caught some after twilight,
my fingers, twigs, shutting out the stars.

ANNIVERSARY IN MARCH

You sent him roses enough for two
at artery's end a heart arrayed,
then kiss for each of your I do's
and wait for Spring up your way.

No purple lilacs beyond the bud
nor crocus flower or stem,
wet snow and hardening mud
and flowerless men and women.

Unbroken clouds are sewn to dusk
and dusk to night is a tailor's dream.
The seed is still beneath its husk
and water freezes at its seams.

MACADAM AND EVE

Men shun me and the women I've known
rise afternoons and circle my dark field.

Fanning the tassels like returning meteors,
they clump in the rows in a search for kernels.
They lie down in the rows and use them like rooms.

They do not take their color from the dusk,
but delight in how they stand out against
the bleached yellow of the stalks like hitchhikers stuck

above the road's controlled horizon.
You've got to check your house
after these flocks have come, even a few fields down,

no matter how many feeders you have. In the kitchen,
rolling the tops off the canisters, she's making dinner
until the window glass gargles a raucous cry.

The sky's got a black top and she's towed
from the door way by the straightening links of their caws.
I've got my thumb out too.

BESTIARY

She dropped me for an animal lover.
At the summer party in the country a squad
of released pigeons marked our arrival.

Kennels kept expensive dogs whose replicas stared
from the glass shelves of a collector. He was
too young to have assembled all this. Upstairs

His parents' banal memorabilia quieted rooms
leased to the afternoon sun. Around the pool
I learned that they roped calves at rodeos,

tackling them is if they had the football. Immense,
he split the water like a dolphin. I swam in a school
of one. Aquariums, painted black below the waterline,

filled their bedroom. Their shower curtain closes
for an examination in a semi-private room. I am
inoperable as she produces a pail of fresh fish he leaps
for, shaking imaginary drops over the table cloth.

REUNION

We'd get together again, you and I
like long unused questions in a history
test, you warily, afraid of my ardor,

I with all the energy of going back
to school. You would have a rock
to stand on while made the earth

my pedestal as always. On the shore
we'd write on tipped shale the old
formulas that got us through the day,

and then run toward a beach ball drifting
from a picnic, pouring over it as
if it were a globe. We'd be as close

as desks, and when it came time to
draw circles I would be bending over
my compass to lodge the tail where

the mouth began, but you, custodian
of so many halos stacked through you
like ripples, would merely reach down

and shuck one, pushing it over your
thighs as if you were undressing
for gym and ten boys were gaping.

FEBRUARY

Winter lay down with me in my drifting bed,
found out my dreams and filled them with snow,
and met me like a wind when I rose for water.

Winter was better than my wife. She matched
my movements, a gust sculpting a hollow
around a tree. Outside cold arms held me,

standing on the ground the frost inhabits.
Bulbs, marooned by her breath, slept beneath.
The gutter, clogged with ice, spilled a long

groove, stopped in the middle of a speech.
My tongue once stuck to a shovel, but I slid
it off with a knife. It burned for days.

I saw myself moving along the lake's margin,
among ice stacked like battery plates.
Fish were out there, wandering in their long cell.

Kicking loose some exposed gravel, I dug
my boot into the beach. Pebbles rattled.
A cloudy sun glared on that wide expanse.
My hands in my pockets, I thought of brides.

WIND

The wind is a gypsy. It ruffles the scarves
of the flowers, then drops over the hill
showing it's back to me like a sunset.

It flies on and returns with winter. Now
it has learned lullabies to brush over the ice
for the eels in the weeds below, lolling as close

as fork tines. The snow is moved with the ease
of ash. The ice appears and disappears as
a scene breathed away by a child's mouth

before a pane. Cattails assembled at the margin
intercede for me, their plush tops robbed
bob in a panic. Fronds divide it but behind

them it rejoins like a couple split on a
crowded sidewalk. I'm there when the ice breaks
up, the pavement shattering in front of me,

brandishing my hands like frantic tridents
to spear this vernal dragon heaving a hundred
mirrors that scatter my visage among the shaking

glass. The wind is a gypsy. It ruffles the scarves
of the flowers, then drops over the hill
showing it's back to me like a sunset.

GRACKLES

What if all this time I have been seeing things
in the wrong light, the rainbows squiggled
in an oiled puddle absent from wrong angle
the grackle attired in an atribilous funereal
coat of many colors blue and purple the hue
of resurrection the meadow brook carrying
the unrinseable pigment of the sky on its surface

TRANSFORMATIONS

Impurities in the glass revise
The accustomed visage of my wife
so through those almost translucent lies
a cheek flares up and she becomes another life
than the one I thought I'd known all along.
This free translation of what lies beneath
distance produces in rendering a stream's clear song,
even misjudging the heights the trees bequeath,
yet I am not dismayed because it's to scale.
The pane's interruptions that continually distort
present me with problems my mind must fail,
until to altered expectations it resorts.
The woman that I knew now seems to wince,
While I stretch between memory and experience.

DIVORCE

Few fruit on the branches hang
which crossed like children's fingers.
For weeks no leaf has lingered,
readier for what the slow wind sang.
The turning crown has got the stars in gangs
whose ancient shapes have spelled out winter.
The wind and grass are down, now nothing hinders
the lake from changing to another language.

I have been left by all in nature. Pebbles
locked in mosaics on the shore are glazed.
The fields in back rebuff me with stubble.
Birds are foreign in the shortening days.
There's nothing here to loosen any trouble.
After clouds and their moon I'm going away.

A CHANGE IN FORECASTING

The bed's four posts, a divided vane, conducted
    the breaths our separate weathers blew;
    and as a farmer stops to view
the storm's approach to see if rough
rain in sheets will interrupt
    ice laid within the furrows as a bruise,
    from our bodies' compass I could deduce
that when north-northeast our passions would erupt.

Now I'm a cloud with shadows still collected,
    silhouettes stacked for a new terrain.
For the sun I've almost intercepted
    I'll return one brighter than Eden's.
There's everything below, and in me resurrected
    are smooth snow kept for fields and brimming rain.

ANIMAL, VEGETABLE, MINERAL, DIVORCE

On a side road near Lake Placid
in the Adirondacks, back when Bud
was king, we split two six packs
playing twenty questions, my brother,
his wife and I. Just enough
of a buzz on to while away the rain
waiting for dinnertime on a summer
weekend. Each had our chain
of questions, logical, memorious,
an edge on the other through
kinship or marriage. A little high,
Sherry laughed as the questions
mounted, a tray of dinners
she waitressed uncrashed
in the Gideon Putnam, a trail
marked as clearly as his proposal,
when he listed the twenty things
he most disliked about her,
then asked for her hand.

ARITHMETIC, THE QUEEN OF MATHEMATICS

If I'm to fall in love again it will only be with numbers.
I could be the royal we in the court of squares.
I'm just a jack of no trades now, rough carpenter
with a plane scrolling a blonde plume of wood
behind the blade. Double me in your mirror.
I need a crown to match your diadem. Finite
bastard, scion of the big bang, desires same.
Solve me for x. Somewhere in the integers'
drift I'll find your dowry. Primes will be
your bridesmaids on an aisle a comet sails.
We'll perform the four operations, galaxies'
grand allemande left, and honeymoon in the digit's
grove on the path of Fermat and Gauss.

THE DIET OF AN INDIVIDUALIST

A boxed lilac studded
with bluebirds, blurred by with her trapeze.
Tights and perfect toes kicking a surcease
of petals, a budded ruckus.

The day more place than time, scudded
on an impressionist frenzy,
memorized from boyhood ecstasy
and dreamed in gardens roosters strut.

Trellised from me in a saffron pagoda,
she trains in a gymnasium
with butterflies, a restive coda
for the afternoon. I close the album
of light with only one photo
the sunset stranding me in magnesium.

PRACTICE

I stood on a ladder under the lilac
as if I could elope with blooms.
The stars ground twilight in a dark pestle
and boxed me in a silver room.

The world beneath me crawled through soil
and dew in ground webs tented down.
The slug inscribed its nightly tune
with a luminous trail to dawn.

Through the sanskrit of its branches
the planets rose as fish,
in the pool where each were golden
I gave them each a kiss.

I tried my courting on the moth
that spells the butterfly,
I pledged my love and plighted troth
with the stream as night went by.

I parted darkened petals to get
nectar on my tongue.
I sent perfume to woo the moon
as if I were the sun.

Alumnus of that lilac dark
degreed in blossoms and spires,
I'd trade its shadow instantly
for proof of your desire.

LUNA

I walked by the sea one moon-night
in the water's uncastling of the sand,
mixing the undertow with my fright

of a life alone, no swell rising into sight
to spread its silver on my waiting land.
I walked by the sea one moon-night

and planks, weeds, shells, stones and kites
in confusion lay upon the strand.
Mixing the undertow with my fright

that none could sink, swim or ride
but were expelled out of hand,
I walked by the sea one moon-night

and caught the moon strapless on the tide
unshored, buoyant in a cold romance.
Mixing the undertow with my fright

that I will never have another bride
to sail with me the wind at our command,
I walked by the sea one moon-night
mixing the undertow with my fright.

THE STRIPPER

Discarding her garments with planned abandon,
her heels so high she drifts across the stage,
with sultry glances she picks out men, random

as a needle that flicks across its gauge.
She flirts behind a fan as red as danger,
and holds the frozen pose that hikes her wage.

The scanty costume that she hands her
customers, they stuff with sulphurous smiles
into their pockets, rising as if in anger

from warm chairs. Her curled hair charms while
she wears the looks a million magazines
display above legs that stretch for miles.

Observations of her, sober, were obscene,
but gin, gaunt on ice and shunted down the throat,
brought taunting thoughts so far from clean
that deckhands dipped their black fists, and wrote
in oil, above pistons grabbing space in greased machines.

MR. AND MRS. WINTER

I see in the icicles the lost consonants,
the portcullis, the confession grill dentals
seethe behind, the drill of runes,
a martinet napoleoned across the rugged eaves,
the code of drips, a letter's dipped vowels,
a stalagmite of correspondence waxing.

Parked at the glaciers lip, you watch for algae
stirred from frost by the sound's breezes,
grounded by a terminal moraine.
I sweep my porch obliquely from mat
to steps, adding a serpentine curve,
leaving a dusting of snow to pollinate.

I put some icicles in the refrigerator,
cold bullion against the warmer days,
the hieroglyphs my study can't contain.
From ribs of old lakes, I can skeleton Eve,
you as a water nymph, blue eyed queen
of melt, raising temperature and desire.

The sky has been a purple blue, choosing
me for this belated winter. Clouds dilute
it, knowing I as unused to such pigments.
Eskers twisting scarve gravel, calligraphy
of giants, and when we walk a stream
together, the blotting ice, the unreasoned

current learning our names but forgetting them
by the next pool, holding our hips for an age,
the clear designs of cold, the draughtsman
finding our way by the stars, snow half way across
to open water, deep, black, resolved,
transits our happiness bend by bend.

AFTER THE RAIN

Upside down anger from an intravenous romance
spills sugar to a meniscus of grief in each
vein. I can level myself, ventriloquist
for a soul to full to speak.

Ether from phlox will last my operation.
Roadsides of it parade my route, but envy
flagellants whose first drops rise with a rain's
readiness. I'll bleed inside and extrude tears.

Valleys sleeping seeds darken under clouds,
shaken by thunder walked by lightning,
want the rustle of wind and the slur of showers,
all day leaves washed, all night their carbons also.

The beetle at the doorstep ticks the screen's squares.
Between lightning and thunder I hold my breath
count in unison. Plotted water warmed
off the mesh relinquishes its gnomon.

CORDON SANITAIRE

Waiting for the thunder after the lightning
my wrist thumbed by a nurse at my pulse
I switch to a second more fulgurant self
as my cumulus clouds start heightening.
Her blood pressure cuff is tightening
around my arm. Brimstone and sulfur
just beyond the window Faust
bargains that couldn't be more frightening.

She takes my oxygen level from a finger
my temperature from a wand in my mouth.
There's no way I can get her to linger
like everyone else she'll go south.
Bad health, no lover, no winter.
I'm left with the devil to rout.

SPRING, LOVE AND GOD

I treat March like a courtship. A plow,
a gang of angel's wings, spills a snow flange
on yellow shoots and love's out of range
until the sun's in a roadside rill, undertow

from a bed of ice, and she's kissing me now.
We're exactly daffodils under the blanket,
old leaves up our sleeves, when an ice storm
unromances us, glassed catkins, to and fro.

And faith's as fickle. The creator retreats
into the corner sulking or kerosenes
from a country lantern while I screen
him from my eyes, blood deep in my heart.
I'm folding my kite, a flag at his funeral,
when a wind comes up with nothing in between.

AS ROOTWORKS WATER-WELDED SWIM FOR THE FIR

As rootworks water-welded swim for the fir
sandals press seamarks sown to the shore.
As fish nets wind thrown fall through the sea,
his love like wells sinks deep in our hearts.
As gases graze candles, as servants say sir,
as crazed grasses like wildfire with mosses make war,
his light on brooks breeds, obeys the dark tree,
suffuses dank mushrooms and mold sought on barks.
All seasons suggest him, for Easter seeds stir,
seduce juice from ice gourds to quiver and soar
to sleek shoots and green knots, and meadows for knees,
and tinder and kindling to harvest the sparks.
To pay the debt of senses that I incurred alone,
I tussle with the rustling husks and tap the root for tone.

THE HORTICULTURALIST

I was the soldier who stood at attention
as you drilled the asparagus in its bed;
you the tin woman with your watering can
waiting for me to pin a heart beneath your head.

You Barnumed heirlooms through their rippling
hoops, better boys, cherry, early girl, and pear.
I was erratic, you were concentric, crippling
with commands an untamable bear.

Your coaxed an elephant from your hutch
etched on the cover of a sterling book
given to your grandfather in India
along with ancient coins he took,

the size I needed for the tiny slots
in the elevator I could not make descend
just the night before in a dream I'd got.
Oneiromancy in romances can't forfend.

I was the vine you could not train,
the scion you could not graft.
The lion undeterred by your chair,
the roughened current around your raft.

You were the windy lass in your faux well
hauling me in buckets to water the garden,
a rain barrel the downspouts swelled
softening the ground water hardened

with minerals, fostering your basil hedge.
Smitten with cumulus and the unlettered stars
you lay on your driveway or stood on a ledge
to let go of nears and grab onto fars.

QUEEN ANNE'S LACE

Forty minutes ago I was among them
as they filled up the hill's stadium,
summer's gawkers at the road's parade.

Their details forgotten by dusk,
they are best then, a slight galactic tilt
giving them an attitude of questioning.

Who has not stuck a finger
into their collapsed umbels,
surprised by their softness
or sniffed this wild carrot,
centering its black dot on their nose.

Antimacassars on parlor chairs,
lamp doilies, or even
my grandmother's pillow cases,
edges lengthened into lace,
waiting in the chest
for my final marriage,
cannot compete.

THE MINE

Tasmania Australia after gold fell dislodging
the miners. Heedless of safety their wives
peered into the pits doving their love calls against
the sides, an empty bucket hauled up in a drought.
Bores and test drillings respectful of the ghost
that tumbled rubble where a floor once stood,
turning the shift and the ore car over and over.
Words mistranslated by the shaft canary notes
miner's lingo the groin of the lode ruptured.
Owners boss cross foreman ore men's losses.
Quarrel over the rescue, rules broken,
danger the third rail skirted and contact made.
At night each wife descends in a basket
filled with picnics, beer, cigarettes,
honeymoon kisses and underwater
embraces and Eurydices her Orpheus,
leaving a stubble of candles to crawl out by,
to squeeze his little ones and hug the boys hello.

MODULATION

The sumac plumes in early July. Dull yellow
cones victorian each tree. Such headdress
a priest would wear when in deep access
to a new world or the hierophantic bellows

of the hedge bindweed, wiring the low
foliage's tedium with its bottomless
pink fringed hoods wind tipped, dew fresh,
a lamplighter's rounds, a taper's glow.

Summer, snuffed by Autumn, smokes.
The poles tilt us to rumination.
The wagon hub revolves its spokes.
We can't cull an instant from the million.
Acorns root underneath their oaks
and underground start a new dominion.

THE GREAT BINDWEED

What keeps the bindweed trumpet at its full,
spread over blackberry bushes like grapes
on trellises, bellowing scent from candle hoods, tapers
lit by an acolyte seed. The climbing green chain
brings the toneless bells with no clappers closer, dull
pink folded by soft geometry. Drapes
knotted tendrils across clinging thorns. Shapes
shrink to their bases, and swell to their rims, lull
by their contours and make my thoughts dim,
shut out my lights and lay me out for sleep,
wheel me in whirlpools that in deep brooks swim
nodding on funnels that sway as they sweep.
Send me to dreams and a wanderer's repose,
deeper than columbine, simpler than rose.

LOST AUTUMN

Much that was beautiful has gone away.
Lit by a taper octagon woods which are
the earth's closets the evening rummages,
have not been found since my earliest frenzy.
Then every leaf carried out its tree's pledge.
Orange stretched to fill the veined route
to tips connecting scallops on the other
side of geometry. Riding the back of a hill
the woods turned in a storm of color
across the iron axis of the bed rock.
In the dry light of autumn the branches
were black vanes leading to leaves each
a direction turned and tuned beyond compass
and composer. Fuller than spring these stopped
colors bunched at the left of the spectrum,
struck their tents and followed wind and soil,
taking me forever, heart and soul.

THE ABDICATION

Bad fall for leaves, rained a lot. Trees are diluted,
futile. Kept last year's around to remind me
what was supposed to happen. Even faded they're
ahead of these. This year's have no imagination.

Colors do not pastel, royal, fauve, sharp or flat.
No large regal glares. Forms are staid, no chances
taken. I saw more trouble in soap stretching
five spectrums across a bottle, each tint a tawdry

wash, heralded to pink, green marked down
regaled by water, and doubled above a blue lagoon.
Nearby a bubble of yellow, palate or oil,
plan or completion, a blueprint few will ever follow,
abandoning the staples of order, not giving a damn.

Yet raking up in one yard was the scarlet bounty
of a solo tree, already two piles of bullion pulled
through dragged tines, and a third being carefully
tossed with just a few rogue yellows deposited
by a poplar which the wind switched for contrast.

I AM THE DEWDROPS
THAT MISS THE DEEP CISTERN

I am the dewdrops that miss the deep cistern
spending themselves on a leaf or a blade.
I am the light in back of the prism
squandering in colors the rigor of rays.
I am the notes arranged on pianos
or alphabets vertical on the page,
feeling too much solace from all the order
of disengaged regiments on parade.
I am the garden in the paper packet,
the undelving trowel in a row of tools.
I am the wind no grasses' racket
rises to mix with from a waving field.
Put me on beaches, rinse me with sand
constantly shifting between sea and land.

I AM AS VAGRANT
AS VINES ON STUCCO

I am as vagrant as vines on stucco
spiraling freely in a vertical plane,
more riotous than the calligraphic ruckus
of brambling roots too curved for canes.
Read me in pages all over October,
my brother wind is tipping the cones.
I freeze the sap and bridle the clover,
shorten the daylight, stop moss on stones.
I am the black prism's untethered shadow,
the turnstile for pebbles in the throat of the falls.
I am the tailor for tomorrow's apple,
the pitchpipe birds use before they call.
I am the pocket where the gloved seed thrusts
watching a halo of planets impart
red rules of living, and how to start
growing even in snow, in ice and in gusts.

TO AND FRO

Tar aches for the return of the roller,
the drum's lullaby, the humid pass
of the asphaltic cylinder glistening
with a radius of oils.

I take up the snail's glutinous passing
by ironing a crease into the shadows,
bumping against the stones as if they buttons.

Behind the mop its path is growing dimmer.

No brush marks.

No refrain.

RESIDUALS

Some subtractions leave unpleasantries.
There's the rest of it, above the bar, the discard.
The moon reduces and we honor her

quarter, the sleeker the better, dieting in
the blue west above the trees, panning
the gold to her rim, darkening her rubble,

and pools, poised traders, maintain
in the face of unending additions,
their equilibrium.

But memory, despite her appetite,
is soon gorged, drops the surcease as sediment,
rounding the bottom,
swelling a silver crescent of tailings.

RESURRECTION

The cemetery's on the left, and lowered
grows verdant cedars dark with private grief.
Its monuments have crouched their awful towers,
on narrow lanes curbed in high relief.

Over all the elms arch mean doors for entry.
The evening flits wayward as an insect.
New graves beyond are opening with a gantry
to descending stairs that allow me to inspect.

Its corners turn me toward a dreamer's grove.
The figment of the bushes covers the genitals of the earth.
Here's a dusk rotation never drove
silent as the cries of my new birth.

A coroner, it's my death I court
west of myself on a street both deep and short.

THE BLOSSOMING CLASS

Never had trouble with the plant before, the north
held enough light for its vine led flowers on porch
or tree, its potted green foliage bloomed to scorch
my tracing fingers. But summer could not bring forth

a single replacement after the florist's initial flourish,
once the fallen limp reds had cooled their torch.
Draped maples had spread spared no shadow scored
each tendrilled leaf with unkindled umbrage, southern

sun playing favorites among the other baskets.
Water and fertilizer were of no effect. I moved
it next to its fecund twin and I asked it
to learn the theorems the other had proved
with such cones dangling that I want my casket
to trail them saying I loved and in return was loved.

WHEN I COME BACK WHAT WILL THE WORLD HAVE LEARNED?

When I come back what will the world have learned?
Will the courageous have shunned war's scourge
covering the graves with flowers; ploughed berms

support a crop of corn? Will tilling tractors turn
a boustrophedon where shells did their worst?
When I come back what will the world have learned?

Will mines have rusted and cluster bomb kerns
rotted beside white phosphorous? Will nature prosper,
covering the graves with flowers? Ploughed berms

in hilly forts make a vista where uranium burned
a path through genes to a generation's disaster?
When I come back what will the world have learned?

Will ammunition that the creeks have churned,
sog its last round, saltpeter pasture?
Covering the graves with flowers ploughed berms

sprout the swords of iris instead of germs
or gas hissed from its unfastened canisters?
When I come back what will the earth have learned?
Graves covered with flowers and ploughed berms?

THE SUN'S ACADEMY

where does the sun go as it slips toward the Solstice
skidding on ice or field glistened clay
in a class it's chained fast sole pupil of heaven
to learn how to make shadows for summer skies
to con the Xray for undressed trees hawks pulpit

to practice reflections in the smallest of pools
that's why it retreats tardier daily
to be checked in the attendance book
marked both present and absent
both late and early in the oldest of schools

or for an advanced class in mirages
Van Goghing south it finds only winter
bare as Belgium in the weeps of February
hoarse for a drink of sacrament light
refreshing its palette in Montmartre

rinsing its brushes in an unlevel brook's
pool shod with blue calcite
pegging its easel against the mistral
paint squeezed from tubes directly on canvas
straw hat woven from Moses' basket's rushes

wind graduating corn by flipping its tassels
the glib hornbook voweled and lettered
the pater noster pasted below we all recite
to bring you back trudging home northed
with paintings warmed with newly found colors

THE NIGHT WAS STOPPED
AT A POTTER'S TABLE

The night was stopped at a potter's table
from which rose a solid cave of clay.
Across the lump was my planet figure able
to eclipse the sun and finally make its way
along a path of sable where I was held in sway

by the countless fortunes of a future diamond ball.
The jar was deepening like a circle digging lantern
whose convex hemispheres shell what sprawls
a shelter of light with hooped tiles of darkness
shingling seamlessly an unwearying hall.

But my murky water eluded its reflection
on whose wan surface rubbed shadows alone.
A hasty exit from the spinning wheel's direction
can make it wobble and take it out of tone.
The bottom drains height slowly from a cone.

Leave quickly, and though she's by your side
an axiomed sadness deducts from mouth to knee
her lack of gesture saying that the ride
was there for you but was not manic spree,
nor were the voice's cords alarmed with radic glee.

So I stayed, a companion of that night
and rounded out the door at a pace for talk
Bearing a compliment I began to walk
full of the freedom felt when you know that light
has finally drawn its shadows and the bedroom door is tight.

I rose up the hill to that damp March street
glistening as if the lights had smoothed it with their melt
to stir him from study or an arcane feat.
When a pebble at the window brought his head I felt
that sturdy promise from which joy is spelt.

He came down the stairs with a soft but steady tread,
breaking the landlord's silence with a door on quiet hinges
to draw in my shadow from what lay beyond its fringes
bringing me to his room where all books were read
so that I could tell how each night wet thing impinges

first on that stream of street whose tar
skids light and thaw to the waiting mouths of drains
carved from curbs or set like suns whose wheeled bars
fray the water loosened by the winter's rains.
Now Spring's unripened annals gain

more anecdotes from our early scans
that force the city's works to take the place
of vernal forests and the blossoming face
of flowers' features whose bulbs still hub their plans.
We set out in a gait that with our minds kept pace,

splashed by the lamps that spoke through the trees' crowns
they turned, stopping to watch a wickless thing kindle
with a flame that we would carry through the town,
owners of the old locales because we regained them grown
in the frames where being, the twin sill

Of function pulled us to her door. The silence let the street alone arrange
for once its houses that came forth so close to walks
that wedged their pooling squares in level chains
with a fervent inanimateness of things that cannot wane,
juggling linked planes that towed the gazer like a pack.

The houses with their owners all in beds
seem immediate as if about to speak,
but on the tips of instants poised instead
their circling cellars and sharpened peaks,
and the spaces that internal timbers bred.

No passersby divided the dimensions,
the unison of the avenue was intact.
The sewers' grates permitted no retention
of the water too shallow to refract
an existence our examination found exact.

How could we carry that brightened pavement
when our journey in night's direction had just begun,
or bear with us the flower budging basement,
keeping with its stones the stories' casements
that in spite of latches towards our bodies swung.

Yet unlike a fair whose booths are all abrupt,
these streetscapes pulled us like an unrelenting curb,
to other houses where ornaments would erupt,
in unwound shapes with motions that disturbed
our habits, and let our hearts disrupt

the regular apprehensions of the often passed scene.
We turned down the hill and toward the older town,
in an homage to its environs' ornate renown
made the smallest thing the object of our dreams,
and surrounded it is if we were its crown.

We were no strangers to its wheels and curves,
expelled in stone, revived with wood and iron,
materials all waiting shapes deserve,
before the chisel, beside the squaring saw,
in a volute, revolved with velocity and with verve.

Additions to its themes each threshold brought,
so much that the concatenations we held,
pillared by each structure where we caught
in the next link the likenesses that had dwelled
unused till now in meters never sought,

stayed through vacant lots or houses all too new
to bring the diagram's design to view.
Fences followed sidewalks and declared
the broken spaces be given all their due,
with respite of turrets that kept the rhythm's cue.

Behind these nether posterns statues steered
their torsos, and took their votive stance,
embodiment of some small deity's creed;
with steady gaze we met his offered glance,
arrested in a moment of a dance.

Whole blocks returned our study and our faith,
by presenting us with friezes where we read
the images on which our journey fed,
in corners round which we'd soon be led,
collecting emblems that would compose the gate,

guarding the entrance to the nocturnal garden,
whose stream was drained through a culvert to a basin,
the only entrance to those who, from that direction,
desired to see its sleeping rows of flowers,
still dreamed in bulbs and in the rooted shapes that tower

in quarters where dark reveries inquire.
We strayed to the core of the oldest district.
This gentle center to which all lanes aspire
slept as a circular lintel liquid with desires.
As wells collect streams and as volcanoes evict

Gathered magma, streets start and end here.
Among them houses had been pushed forward
like watchers jostling for a late parade.
The clapboards edged on sidewalks and laid
the dwellers' rustlings just beyond our ears.

Like scythes just off a sharpening wheel
we recoiled, our dullness traded for near
vertigo, and inevitable as magnets,
learned a lane sloping to a rising river.
The house that turned us round the corner,

whose windows, bright on four main levels,
rose up from sills like rims of pots lifted
from their bases, kept a garden muffled
by a stuccoed wall, through whose gate's small grill
we saw unleafed lattices, stakes bundled,

snow on raised plots, brick walks, locked sheds,
iced benches and a frozen fountain. Like
a mother who has seen unharmed and sleeping
her child in his room onerous with dreams,
we slowly left to a season in slumber

flowers untroweled still trammeled in seeds.
Below the houses we met an algid coil
brimming with night water, a goblet ready
at bedside. Its sinuous path, mime of the currents,
caught us with gestures and would leave us like a wind.

A sparse grove lifted wet black branches
in letters found within an alphabet
long as a hedge. Ice crammed at the river's
margins would by reflection have memorized
those characters bristling with nocturnal syntax
that joined the rim of trees into arboreal
sentences in whose paragraph we were two
objects, but the immobile facets of the serpentine
diamond slept in square scales beyond the still
unfruited trees, whose limbs thrown up and out
danced the basic thrill of unstopped knots at length.

We labored in the center and walking around
saw branches crossing like promises until
again untangled, they framed the space they knew.
Like figures climbing out of clay half caught,
like backward swimmers towed in a thrown
tide, struggling like vast squid whose vagrant
arms boil with motion, the trees seethe, waving
above black waists gray saxes lengthened through
penumbral octaves. Plural melodies wait, anxious
as words to express an aria, throng a threnody.
Throats welling up from roots rehearse a still
trillion, release black stacks of bumpy circles
perpetuated into limbs at the rate the earth's
collected smiles flee from every living visage.
Rival beings, whose strenuous souls are
omnivorously devoured by a woody ubiquity,
admit us to your circle so that we can stand,
magisterially impervious to habit and opinion,
ready to greet being as a poet accepts
a dislodged stone, in perpetual forgetfulness
continually surprised. For every root below
a limb above rises in answer, trading
snails for stars. For every branch sectioning
off the sky, a pronged root divides plots juggling
constellations of boulders, nether magnitudes
charting low waters, the conglomerations
by which slugs correct their course. These chthonic
mariners steer through quadrants as easily
as stars, and are as organized.
In us this nether zoo had reached a silent zenith
as insistently onerous as leaves, and its order
wasn't ours. As animals crowd around a distant
waterhole in a time of drought we hunched
over an illiterate well whose bricks were
guiding its waters to a gushing fountain
too wide for consonants, too quick for vowels.
No matter that we stopped, the stream still sped,
since wherever we looked the thing churned

in the thronged stream or if we closed our eyes
the images rushed the same calling like friends
we never knew, returning to a home they'd never
left. Like a starred shape a blend of flower
and animal pastured and blooming in a fecund heaven,
that knew love and lost it, and urged a rubicund
ululation, shrieked a shrill shoot, kept the electric
friction, a susurrant ruckle huddled in its antelope
heart until it surged faster than geometry
through the lineaments of his frame watered by
the Hyades, and sub vocal now searched like lightning
for an alphabet to sound in, we were the planets where
each thing could unleash its accumulated lightnings,
heave its huge hail now grown to the size of granite.
We felt the verbs in the sleeping forms ignite,
be all their boundaries budged. He worked
the ponderous chords the organ in the church
he named Jung's castle would have thronged like mulch
under the roots of our being. He'd read the myths
and brought them on this trip, spread them like maps
on the route we were making famous, so that even
now at corners or a trine of brick led streets
ancestral archetypes gather and animus retreats.
Now we were headed for our college's largest garden
whose stream fed pipe's imminent mouth yawns,
an antrum. Retaining walls we passed were tilted,
bulging with a promise of frost a load too large
to share entirely. Things watched us as if
we were marching and again the static solids
of the buildings coruscated in planes and colors
as counterpoint to the earlier melodies. At the pipe's
mouth we bent as if over fire and climbed
onto the lip that started one long vowel.
The corrugations ribbed it and we went underground
rubbing our knees against the watered hoops
through the stack of double arches,
our voices shifted as the warming night.
We saw the circles as arcs and their

reflections half risen suns mired in
the horizon's mud scooping salamanders
and crystals. Night birds active in the moon's
ceilings prophesized above us and we raised,
already ascending to the zenith, our hopes
for the garden I had guarded by a locked gate.
Night light on snow bloomed in a circle
and soon we were where the pipe swallows
strenuous stream and we came out under

Eden. Trees, matching the streams of soporific
rhythm spread as if we were the first
inhabitants. Groves gathered in search of a God,
as we hallowed them as passing divinities.
We created what we saw.

Everything wanted names and we turned
to bough, branch and twig and made them equal
with their kind outside. A slide of instants
to a junction all of whose choices are true and
used. We heard the bulbs revolve

arrayed in patterns under a dress of snow.
They will flick their blooms like lighters, but we will
pass from bed to bed settling the quarrel
of leaf and flower with lines woven
upon the hour with the sun and moon in tow.

We advance under clouds illumed
by streetlights and neons on prominent
corners left in a neighborhood exhumed
by our walks, proving the pavement
flags us, all objects, bride and bridegroom

in being what they are and the verb to act.
We have another business to transact
than following the trades of our elders.
Spring lodged in untaught trees tells
us the season of the present tense backs

through each stone, clatters down a riser
in a stair. The streams ripples sold their
cool rings to shale and the wooden bridge
loomed in the lower garden where flute
and sax joined poems tumble fresh as falls.

DESTINOS

Once I could walk in and find Liz fresh off
some painting brightened from her palette
of the woods that surged behind her sewing factory
and kitchen on Pitt Road ready for a margarita
or Angela head full of madonnas and easels
just in from her villa on the Kinderhook
thick with fruit trees, vined flowers, vegetables
two minutes from the table, stocked with pasta, cat,
psychology books and spirit, whose annual summer
party drew the creative together over chicken
and grilled pears, or Buffy, who could massage
without touching and fill you with the good
from her overflowing soul, or Liseli, who also
worked at Powell House, the gentlest nurse
I ever knew, the both of them helping me
Into my clothes after a knee operation,
or Nan, masseur, the latest arrival, who opened
her home one night to all to find the friends
one needs when so new to a locale, all Quakers,
all moved away one by one from where I eat alone.

ANN

It has been snowing for a half hour while still dark
I shined a flashlight out the window and it was falling
in a slant the scant leaves told no wind so I ruled
out rain, and not hail nor sleet either at the end
of October after a day of soaking rain to bring the wells
up and now it is light and despite my lamp's reflection
in the window I can see the flakes falling between
our houses filling the space to the trees backed
by the fence the second raking not yet done
leaves sodden give up pressed to the ground
their colors traded for browns including the cherry's
and now the storm is thickening and the trees
beyond the fence are blurred cedar, pine and spruce
with respect to their distances and the bush
that still retains its leaves is being coated
on which the birds perch now flocking to the feeders
and the leaves are bedding down the snow
that the gravel driveway still melts so it has made
one friend again but who can replace Ann who
died this week in her son's arms my Quaker
friend for years we drove each other and talked
along the way set up for the pot lucked movies
I took her to the classical concerts in Kinderhook
she'd buy me lunch in the café down from the church
Mozart Beethoven Hummel Handel Bach and Haydn
where Vicky's husband conducted the orchestra
and Sandy, Vicky and Noah sang in the chorus
she had a piano in her house and played a wind
instrument and bridge we worked on book sales
fundraisers for our meetinghouse she lifting
boxes my back could not and sorting them into
categories other Quakers would dispute, the same
book moving among disciplines over several days
she'd give me pens after I started writing poems
in meeting for worship and a sweater she'd knitted

one night in the dark and snow she fell on the stone
steps huge slate they'd lifted all together on her hands
and knees somehow still holding her dish it had snowed
then too and it was slippery and dangerous just the two
of us always arriving early she was quite prompt
we worked the jazz concerts together she at the door
collecting money and presold tickets which had got printed
she made many arrangements for our county fair
exhibit of the solitary confinement cell replica two
years running and sat with me to explain to passersby
why the hearts of men and women deadened in that hole
she had a fine sense of humor and the prettiest face
with a warm smile her daughter and granddaughter shared
attended national Quaker conferences and would speak
of a gathered meeting always brought the bagels
helped families in need without asking questions
she was kind and a good listener with great stories
taught me words too long for me to have remembered
we talked of flowers and bushes that bloom in spring
she loved to read both heavy and light and she'd give
me Jack Reacher novels we would sit in the car before
taking her home and she'd look out into the field behind
the meeting house the wheels of hay rolled up
on the almost drumlin trees behind fine in any
season and exclaim the beauty of the view
now the snow is weighing down my yew
roofs have whitened and I'm frightened all alone
my throat constricted I wished I'd called her more
but many times we talked just on the phone
the rain in my eyes I wish would change to snow
so I could blink and see where I'm to go

CANCER ROUND III

Let us go then, you and I,
when the evening is spread out against the sky,
like a patient etherized upon the table. T.S. Eliot

I told a woman at the radiation treatment center
that I had warmed up the table for her.
We cannot have a sheet, blanket, mattress or pad
under us because staff have to eliminate any
variables that will affect the calibration
and positioning of the arms that wheel
over us burning their beneficent invisible
passage through our skin to the cancer.
The hardness of the table and the head rest
and in the case of thyroid, throat and brain
malignancies the plastic helmet they clamp
on our faces, through whose colander
holes we breathe, our shoulders buckled in,
fit us to be cosmonauts within our planetarium,
blue lights screaming through the smallest
of apertures. We swallow just before
the mask is lowered should both nostrils ever
close we can guppy scant air through our mouths.
We clasp the rubber ring across our chests
on the fair ride we were dare deviled into.
We are aligned perfectly for the mortuary.
Retractable as the longest of drawers.
About half way into it swallowing becomes
painful, and I'm told to call the pharmacy never
again do I try to take two pills at once, choker
scar where the second operation was aborted,
fill line on a measuring jar, hoarser than ever.
Powdered fine enough I'll snort them like cocaine.

Grate on their scrannel pipes of wretched straw, John Milton

ACKNOWLEDGEMENTS

POEM	PUBLISHED BY
Against Sleep's Gymnasts	Dirigible
Allee Allee In Free	Sylvia
Asylum	Orphic Lute
Change Of Diet	Bogg
Divorce	Piedmont Literary Review
Wonder	Piedmont Literary Review
Exits And Entrances	Footprints
February	Twilight Ending
General Delivery	Writers Exchange
Hipboots	The Electric Acorn
I Am A Star Without Astronomers	Re:Al-Stephen F. Austin State University
I Don't Need A Choir	Poets Attic Quarterly
Icarus After The Fall	Wavelength
Icarus: If I Could Fly Again...	Vallum
Infidelity	Cedar Rock
It's Twins	Pemmican
Jaywalking	Dirigible
Mr. Wizard	Fauquier

POEM	PUBLISHED BY
Population Explosion	The Little Magazine
Somewhere Between The Stars And Snails	Snail's Pace
The Accumulation	Troubadour
The Comet	Sunstone
The Education Of Desire	Great Midwestern Quarterly
The Foundling	No Exit
The Haruspex	Blind Man's Rainbow
The Marble Pit	California Quarterly
The Monologue	Peer Glass
The Naturalist	Spelunker Flophouse
The Proposal	Writers Journal
The Renaissance Man	Re:Al-Stephen F. Austin State University
The Sun Droops Lower In The West	Bitter Root
White Chocolate, Lies...	Dionysia Press Understanding Magazine
Solstice	LittleStar
Fireflies	LittleStar
Parthenogenesis	LittleStar
The Horticulturalist	LittleStar
Making My Bed	Friend's Journal